MW00624131

DAVENANT GUIDES seek to offer short and accessible introductions to key issues of current debate in theology and ethics, drawing on a magisterial Protestant perspective and defending its contemporary relevance today.

JESUS AND PACIFISM

An Exegetical and Historical Investigation

BY ANDREW A. FULFORD

CONTENTS

I:
CONTEXT

"BUSH lied, people died." I came of age politically and intellectually during the presidency of George W. Bush. As a self-proclaimed Christian evangelical, the president's statements and decisions provoked countless arguments and discussions among my friends about the relationship of Christians to the state. During my years as an undergraduate, I encountered and studied the works of both Drs. Oliver O'Donovan and John Howard Yoder, along with some of Dr. Yoder's most renowned students (like Drs. Stanley Hauerwas and Richard Hays), and for a time Dr. Yoder convinced me of his version of Christian pacifism. At that time, for an evangelical who was concerned about obedience to scripture, he seemed to have the stronger exegetical case. Many of my friends agreed, and defenders of his basic position continue to publish books today.[1]

However, I was not satisfied in his camp for very long. As time went on, I began to have questions that Dr. Yoder did not satisfactorily answer for me, and yet neither did his contemporary anti-pacifist critics. These questions included the significance of the Old Testament (hencefor-

---

[1] A recent example would be Preston Sprinkle, *Fight: A Christian Case for Non-Violence* (Colorado Springs: David C. Cook, 2013).

ward abbreviated "OT") for Christian ethics, the place of natural law in the same, and the precise details of some Yoderian exegesis. At the same time as these questions arose for me, I was also studying issues of biblical authority, hermeneutics, and early church history, and all those studies inevitably coloured my thoughts on the other areas.

Being satisfied neither with Dr. Yoder nor with the already published criticisms of his work, I began to look for cognitive rest on the issue by studying the sources directly and with biblical commentators and church historians (rather than primarily Christian ethicists). The answers I give here are the results of that search. I have developed some of the arguments present here even further than they appear in this work, and hope to write something more comprehensive on the subject in the future. For the time being, however, since interest in the subject is not waning, and because I haven't seen any other work that answers the questions I had in a way that satisfies me, I offer them to other readers who might be on a similar search for answers.

This book originally made its appearance as a series of posts at *The Calvinist International*, and has been lightly edited and supplemented for this new publication. When I originally conceived the series, I decided that the clearest way to tackle the issue would be to focus on the teachings of Jesus, and to address pacifism as an historical hypothesis. I still think this way of approaching the question is the best, given my purposes. This way of ingression was partly motivated by the audience I was attempting to engage, and still hope to reach. In my experience, many Christian pacifists have a stronger commitment to following Jesus than to the authority of scripture *per se*. My argument was—and is—an attempt to have a conversation with that demographic on common ground. To this end, I treat the OT and the NT outside of the "Red Letters" primarily as documents that provide the historical context to Jesus' teaching, rather than as authoritative as such. Thus, this book will attempt to come at an interpretation of Jesus' teaching in a kind of pincer movement, from the direction of both its background context and its foreground interpretation. Following this survey, it will provide a positive exposition of Jesus' teaching in accord with theses contexts. Finally, it will offer several possible causes that could explain how the early church slid from Jesus' teaching to a more stringently pacifistic stance.

Four contexts provide the backdrop against which Jesus presents his views: natural law, literary practices, social setting, and the Old Testament.

It is important to begin our analysis of Jesus' teaching with his background context, because it is this context that he would have shared with his original hearers. One of the basic rules of hermeneutics, a rule Dr. Martin Joos called "Semantic Axiom Number One," is the principle of relevance. This principle dictates that "the best meaning is the least meaning."[2] More explicitly, it states that communicators will assume common context with their audience, and will attempt to convey a message in the most economical means they can.

From one perspective, this hermeneutical rule is simply an application of Ockham's razor: in attempting to explain the meaning of a communication, we should

---

[2] Martin Jones, "Semantic Axiom Number One," in *Language* 48 (1972): 256-265.

postulate the fewest causes (of meaning) we can. If we can explain all the details of a text with the words themselves and with two contextually assumed ideas, that interpretation is preferable to one which requires we assume three contextual ideas.

With this point in mind, we can begin to look at what ideas were "in the air", available to both Jesus and his hearers, when he first spoke his words.

NATURAL LAW

At the *Calvinist International* I have argued that Jesus appealed to natural law as authoritative in his own teaching;[3] this argument will appear in a forthcoming book as well, but in the meantime I will assume that previous argument and proceed accordingly. I have contended that Jesus assumed natural law existed, that it was binding, and that his audience knew it. In light of this, it is fair to ask: what does this law teach about matters of violence and war?

First, Aristotle argued,[4] rightly, that nature directs man towards forming both family and political community. His argument was essentially that human beings cannot survive as isolated individuals, and that they flourish when they live in community. For this reason, he

---

[3] See the final post here, which contains links to the earlier installments: "An Exegetical Case for Natural Law: Concluding Thoughts," The Calvinist International, May 24, 2013,

https://calvinistinternational.com/2013/05/24/an-exegetical-case-for-natural-law-concluding-thoughts/ (accessed September 26, 2016).

[4] Aristotle, *Politics*, Book 1.

[5] See my post, "Zanchi on What Natural Law Teaches," The Calvinist International, May 6, 2013, https://calvinistinternational.com/2013/

called man a political animal, in that human nature as such directs people towards life in the *polis* as its natural end. Within this general trajectory, the freedom open to human beings allows for different ways for communities to govern themselves, but most often communities tend to choose to have representative rulers of some kind.

Second, throughout history, most natural law thinkers[5] have recognized that the natural order directs animals toward self-preservation, and self-defense. When we recognize that the "self" in human life expands beyond the individual, as people have property and loved ones they also regard as in some way bound up with their own flourishing, the right to self-defense extends to the right to defend others. Again, this is basically taken as common sense throughout the world. It is important to note that "defense" here is not necessarily an amoral concept, nor is it necessarily physically passive. Rather, defense is aimed at the preservation of natural goods, and so shares in that natural goodness. Hugo Grotius writes in two sections of *The Rights of War and Peace* I.II.I:

> 1. Hence comes it, says [Cicero], that there's no Man left to his Choice, who had not rather have all the Members of his Body perfect and well shaped, than maimed and deformed. And that is the first Duty of every one to preserve himself in his natural State, to seek after those

---

[5] See my post, "Zanchi on What Natural Law Teaches," The Calvinist International, May 6, 2013, https://calvinistinternational.com/2013/05/06/zanchi-on-what-natural-law-teaches/ (accessed on August 13, 2016).

Things which are agreeable to Nature, and to avert those which are repugnant.[6]

3. ... Among the first Impressions of Nature there is nothing repugnant to War; nay, all Things rather favour it: For both the End of War (being the Preservation of Life or Limbs, and either the securing or getting Things useful to Life) is very agreeable to those first Motions of Nature; and to make use of Force, in case of Necessity, is in no wise disagreeable thereunto; since Nature has given to every Animal Strength to defend and help itself.[7] ...

But Right Reason, and the Nature of Society ... does not prohibit all Manner of Violence, but only that which is repugnant to Society, that is, which invades another's Right: For the Design of Society is, that everyone should quietly enjoy enjoy his own, with the Help, ... and by the united Force of the whole Community.[8]

This brings us directly to the issue of punishment. And here, too, we find that basically all the cultures of the world have recognized that punishment is a just and necessary form of behaviour in appropriate circumstances. It consists of giving to people what they deserve (the

---

[6] Hugo Grotius, *The Rights of War and Peace* (Indianapolis: Liberty Fund, 2005), 180, http://oll.libertyfund.org/titles/grotius-the-rights-of-war-and-peace-2005-ed-vol-1-book-i (accessed on October 14, 2016).

[7] Grotius, 182-183.

[8] Grotius, 184.

definition of justice in general) when they deserve to hurt, because they have injured others. Prof. C.S. Lewis describes this view of punishment:

> [T]he concept of Desert is the only connecting link between punishment and justice. It is only as deserved or undeserved that a sentence can be just or unjust. I do not here contend that the question 'Is it deserved?' is the only one we can reasonably ask about a punishment. We may very properly ask whether it is likely to deter others and to reform the criminal. But neither of these two last questions is a question about justice. ... On the old view the problem of fixing the right sentence was a moral problem. Accordingly, the judge who did it was a person trained in jurisprudence; trained, that is, in a science which deals with rights and duties, and which, in origin at least, was consciously accepting guidance from the Law of Nature, and from Scripture. We must admit that in the actual penal code of most countries at most times these high originals were so much modified by local custom, class interests, and utilitarian concessions, as to be very imperfectly recognizable. But the code was never in principle, and not always in fact, beyond the control of the conscience of the society. And when (say, in eighteenth-century England) actual punishments conflicted too violently with the moral sense of the community, juries refused to convict and reform was finally brought

about. This was possible because, so long as we are thinking in terms of Desert, the propriety of the penal code, being a moral question, is a question in which every man has the right to an opinion, not because he follows this or that profession, but because he is simply a man, a rational animal enjoying the Natural Light.[9]

Third, following from these general principles, the classical tradition rightly derived fairly obvious consequences, distilled into the just war tradition. There are many ways of listing the criteria of a just war, but two distinct categories have fixed themselves into the tradition: criteria for whether someone should go to war (*jus ad bellum*), and criteria for how a war should be conducted (*jus in bello*). For the purposes of this survey, only the first set need be discussed, and only three of the criteria within that category.

From the fact that the common good represents the highest temporal end of human activity, it follows that whatever acts individual and communities perform must be for the common good. But from this follows the axiom that no one should act when the foreseeable effects of an act will cause more harm than good. This is the just war criterion of reasonable prospect of success. Further, the obligation to act for the good of others entails that no one should harm another person unless they deserve it, in which case such actions would take the form of punishment, an expression of justice; in general, people should do

[9] C.S. Lewis, "The Humanitarian Theory of Punishment," in *God in the Dock* (1970; Grand Rapids: W.B. Eerdmans, 2014), 319-320.

good to their fellow human beings. This intuition is summarized in the criterion of just cause. These two points entail a third. In general, political authorities are only such if they possess enough force to overpower any given threat from their subjects (though not necessarily from their entire body politic). In modern terms, they must have a monopoly on violence. The result of this aspect of governments is that the chances of revolutionaries successfully overthrowing the rulers is less probable than failure. Of course, sometimes exceptions happen, but as a general rule, governments are the most powerful force in a given state. In light of this general reality, prudence directs subjects to remain subordinate to their rulers. And the political nature of human beings more directly leads to this conclusion: people should act in community, and insofar as a government represents a community, members should act in accord with their own government. (Of course, there can be exceptional situations when a government becomes unbearably tyrannical, when it clearly is no longer acting for the common good. But this is not always the case.) This entails the third relevant *jus ad bellum* criteria: wars should be waged by legitimate authorities, by governments and those they have deputized, not by private actors.

The natural created order, then, provides reason for there to be governments that use coercion, and for subjects to remain subject to them, including in not taking that coercion into their own hands. This provides one context for Jesus' teachings.

LITERARY PRACTICES

A second context comes in the literary customs deployed in the writing and interpretation of law. In the context of his interpretation of Jesus' teaching on divorce, Dr. Craig Keener writes:

> It was perfectly natural in Matthew's day to suppose that any law would need to be qualified; that there were exceptions to general rules which would need to be articulated was simply assumed. For instance, Quintilian, a famous Roman rhetorician of the first century, cites a Roman law but proceeds to show that exceptions are implicit within it: "'Children shall support their parents under penalty of imprisonment.' It is clear, in the first place, that this cannot apply to an infant. At this point we turn to other possible exceptions and distinguish as follows." Quintillian's book is about rhetoric and he was thus making the sort of argument that lawyers would have used when they approached legal texts.[10]

This principle of allowing for unstated exceptions also applied outside of strictly legal contexts, in the genre of "wisdom":

> Wisdom sayings, as one gathers quickly from the book of Proverbs, are general principles stated in a succinct manner designed to grab the reader's attention and to make a point. But wisdom sayings do not exhaust all that is to be said on a subject, nor did anyone sup-

---

[10] Keener, Craig, S., *And Marries Another: Divorce and Remarriage in the Teaching of the New Testament* (Peabody: Hendrickson Publishers, 1991), 27.

pose that they did. For instance, Proverbs often speaks of wealth as God's blessing; just as often, however, it condemns wealth acquired by evil means. It is not that some wisdom sayings in Proverbs contradict other wisdom sayings; rather, each states a general principle, and most principles would need to be qualified if we were to try to enforce them in every situation.[11]

When Jesus made statements like he did in the Sermon the Mount, then, he spoke into a context where people would assume general rules could have unstated exceptions.

We should not overlook that this principle is not a curiosity of first century Rome or Judea. Rather, this is a general convention of human communication, and in fact is an expression of Semantic Axiom Number One. People do not explicitly state things that they regard as obvious, or as assumed by their audience; to make such explications on every occasion would be needlessly onerous.

SOCIAL SETTING

A third context for Jesus' teaching was his social setting, and that of his listeners. More explicitly: Jesus spoke as a man without political power to people who were mostly without political power. That this was true of Jesus is obvious, but a little reflection can show it is also true of his audience. First, First-Century Palestine was a client kingdom, ruled by the Herods, on behalf of the Roman Emperor. Even within the government, then, the number

---

[11] Keener, 24-25.

of people who had power was actually quite small. There was no democracy functioning here. Second, in general, representative governments (and all governments claimed to be representative) are smaller in population than the mass of subjects they govern. These two reasons together imply that, if Jesus drew crowds, the average person in those crowds would not have any role as a public representative, with a correlative right to exercise coercion. They were all (at least in general) private citizens.

THE OLD TESTAMENT

The *locus classicus* of pacifist proof-texts is the Sermon on the Mount. The nearest context to this purported teaching contains an important interpretive guardrail for all of Jesus' teachings: Matt. 5:17: "Do not think that I have come to abolish the Law or the Prophets; I have not come to abolish them but to fulfill them."[12] While we will discuss the meaning of this text further on, the *prima facie* sense of it implies we must at least consider the OT context of Jesus' words when discerning their intention. Further, even if Jesus had not made this statement, his context would demand it: Jesus was a faithful Jew, speaking as a religious teacher; everyone listening would have knowledge of the OT law, and thus it forms part of the context of his words.

So we can turn to those scriptures and consider whether he is echoing OT teachings. And when we do this, we find that he is. The OT commands subjects to submit to their rulers (Prov. 24:21-22), though not

---

[12] All quotations are taken from the English Standard Version, unless otherwise noted.

unconditionally,[13] and prohibits murder (which, usually, is motivated by anger and so is a way of taking natural justice into one's own hands). Dr. Charles E. Carlston rhetorically asks, stressing the perennial nature of the proverb, "[a]nd who first said–or last applied–the truth that 'All who take the sword will perish by the sword'?" He gives the OT example of Prov. 22:8, and outside of the OT, Sirach 27:25-27; Homer, *Odyssey* 16.294; and Pindar, *Nemean Odes* 4.32).[14]

---

[13] E.g., 1 Sam. 14:43-45, and countless texts which make clear that loyalty to God must overrule loyalty to king when they are in conflict.

[14] Charles E. Carlston, "Proverbs, Maxims, and the Historical Jesus," *JBL* 99, no.1 (1980): 100. Dr. W.D. Davies and Dr. Dale C. Allison note further regarding this idea:

> Perhaps proverbial, a piece of folk wisdom. The form, which recalls the *lex talionis* and NT's so-called sentences of holy law, is in any event thoroughly conventional. We recall m. Abot 2:7: Hillel said: 'Because you drowned (others) they drowned you' (probably of Pompey). Cf. also Prov 22:8; Hos 10:13; Ecclus 27:27; Rev 13:10a. (Davies and Allison, *A Critical and Exegetical Commentary on the Gospel According to Saint Matthew*, vol. 3, *International Critical Commentary*, (New York: T & T Clark, 2004), 512n51)

> The words remind one both of Gen 9:6 ('Whoever sheds the blood of man, by man shall his blood be shed') and Tg. Isa. 50:11 ('Behold, all you that kindle a fire, that take a sword, go, fall into the fire you have kindled and on the sword you have taken. From my Memra you have this: you shall return to your destruction'). (Davies and Allison, 512)

Dr. John Nolland writes of other relevant texts: "E.g., Ps. 7:15 (in terms of digging a pit and falling into it); Pr. 26:27 (as Ps. 7:15, but also in terms of setting a stone rolling down a hill); Ec. 10:8 (as Ps. 7:5); Is. 50:11 (in terms of those who set destructive fires); Sir. 27:26 (as Ps. 7:5)." *The New International Greek Commentary: The Gospel of Matthew* (Grand Rapids: Eerdmans, 2005), 1113.

It also commands private citizens to treat their enemies lovingly.[15] Further, it assumes it is possible for normal human beings to determine the guilt of others in a legal situation (Deut. 13:12-15; 17:2-7; 21:18-21; 22:22; 25:1-3), and that punishment was a permissible kind of action for normal people to perform (Deut. 13:6-9). More specifically, it affirmed that normal judges could determine when capital punishment was an appropriate sentence, and that the sentence could be carried out (Deut. 13:6-9; 16:18-20),[16] but prohibited private citizens from killing (Deut. 5:17; Lev. 19:18).[17] It also taught that coercive punishment could effectively deter future lawlessness (Deut. 13:11; 17:13). Further, the OT law clearly was aimed at dealing with serious injuries (Ex. 21:23; Lev. 24:17-21), not with trivial harms like insults (Lev. 19:17-18).[18]

---

[15] Pr. John Day notes this is commanded in Ex. 23:4-5 and Prov. 25:21-22, and exemplified in 2 Kings 5-6. He adds: "While it must be granted that the command to 'love your enemies' is nowhere to be found in the Old Testament, the concept 'cannot be confined to the words themselves. When enemies are fed and cared for, rather than killed or mistreated, love for enemy is being practiced.'" John Day, *Crying for Justice: What the Psalms Teach us about Mercy and Vengeance in an Age of Terrorism* (Grand Rapids: Kregel Publications, 2005), 88.

[16] The people are gathered here, which suggests public approval of the punishment.

[17] For these two passages to be consistent with the rest of the OT law code, they must be about private citizens, not public officials.

[18] The instruction not to take vengeance or hold a grudge, but to reason with your brother and show love, implies an expectation that some "injuries" could be sufficiently dealt without outside the system of law, and no doubt these were injuries of less severity. Dr. Greg Welty's essay, "The Eschatological Fulfillment and Confirmation of Mosaic Law: A Response to D.A. Carson and Fred Zaspel on Matthew 5:17-48," alerted me to this aim of the OT Law. It can be found online at Analogical Thoughts: The Virtual Home of James N. Anderson, March 28, 2002, http://www.proginosko.com/welty/carson.htm (accessed on August 13, 2016).

It is worth noting that many of these statements stand side by side with laws and narratives that suggest limits, as I noted briefly regarding the general obligation to obey rulers. Further, it should be obvious that the commands to love one's enemies were not meant to contradict commands directing the community to go to war, or to punish murderers, even though qualifications are not explicitly given in the immediate context of either of these kinds of texts.

The principle of charity dictates that we should attribute as much coherence as possible to the words of others, taking into account common context. As a general rule of communication, it applies just as much to ancient writings as it does today, and thus Moses wrote assuming we would apply it to his words. Certainly, by the time of Jesus, Moses' words were considered absolutely authoritative and true; all of Jesus' contemporaries would assume all texts related to the ethics of violence would be consistent on final analysis. This is not only because they followed the principle of charity, but also because they regarded the text as the word of God, and so undoubtedly beyond the possibility of internal inconsistency.

TYPES OF PACIFISTIC RATIONALES

With these principles found in the Law, along with the three contexts noted above (including especially the natural law context, which the Old Testament law essentially republishes on this subject) we can return to our central subject of pacifism. The first thing that must be acknowledged when analyzing a thing like pacifism is that there is not just one kind. Rather, many rationales are offered by different individuals and traditions for a common practical end, that of nonviolence.

This means that any attempt to determine whether a position is pacifist, or to refute pacifism, is more complicated than one might anticipate. However, one useful way to classify the position is based on scholastic types of law. Aquinas famously subdivided law into four categories: eternal, natural, human, and divine. The first category is not relevant to our question, as it is too broad: it refers to the order that the entire universe participates in, including inanimate and sub-rational creatures. Further, human law is not relevant, since we are seeking the answer to a moral question, and since human law has clearly not been pacifist in many cases. Rather, the kinds of pacifism we are interested in come in two major varieties: those based on an appeal to natural law, and those that appeal to divine positive law.[19]

In my encounters with pacifistic advocates, I have encountered six recurring arguments for absolute non-violence that fall under the category of natural law arguments. They are:

The Cycle of violence: violence always provokes further violence, and so never really solves anything.

The Limits of human knowledge: human beings can never truly determine the guilt of another person, and so coercive judgment can never be verified as just.

---

[19] Though he does not use this classification, John Howard Yoder's *Nevertheless: The Varieties of Religious Pacifism* (Waterloo, Ontario: Herald Press, 1992) is probably the best work to make clear the widely variegated rationales that traditions have offered throughout history for pacifistic practice. The different flavours he discusses could be divided into my two categories, but for the sake of brevity I will avoid doing so.

The Immorality of punishment and vengefulness: the very idea of retribution and vengeance are immoral and barbaric,

The Unloving character of violence: violence is inconsistent with the virtue of love.

The Utopian character of violence: violence can never truly achieve real justice or common good, even while claiming that it can.

Hierarchy as intrinsically dominative: any sort of hierarchy is unjust intrinsically, and thus so too for one person to punish someone under his or her authority.

One characteristic that each of these arguments have in common is that they all imply pacifism is trans-historically mandatory. That is, because they appeal to aspects of reality that remain true across redemptive history, they must imply that non-violence has always been ethically obligatory.

And then there is the other kind of rationale for pacifism, the one based on divine positive law. In this kind of position, the reason for non-violence is not strictly moral; rather, it is based on divine fiat, a suspension of the natural order in favor of a transcendent grace. The reason for prohibiting violence does not derive from the nature of human beings, nor of the current state of the created order (including the presence of evil), as such, but rather derives strictly from an additional divine command given in history, the new law of the gospel. With this kind of rationale, pacifism need not be ethically mandatory in every age, but it is nonetheless binding for Christians and an essential element of the New Covenant order.

What all these arguments have in common is a specific conclusion. They all entail, at minimum, that no

Christian can participate in the state use of violence, especially in the form of killing another person. The moral/natural approaches entail a stronger conclusion: that no one could rightly participate in such activity at all.

The next section will discuss how the Old and New Testaments both affirm the content of the context mentioned in the previous section, and then will determine whether any of these pacifistic arguments, and thus pacifism in general, are consistent with that content.

II:
COMPARING THE OLD AND NEW TESTAMENTS

THE OLD TESTAMENT AND PACIFISM

WE HAVE already discussed how natural law rules out any type of moral or transhistorical pacifism. But now the foregoing analysis of the varieties of pacifism provides us with the ability to measure the consistency of pacifism with the OT. The survey of the OT data above shows the Hebrew Bible contradicts these arguments for pacifism. "Cycle of violence" arguments contend that violence never solves anything, but only provokes more violence. But the OT believes that the death penalty for idolatry will deter people from continuing to practice it. It affirms the efficacy of state coercion to control the behaviour of subjects. The "limitation of knowledge" approach contradicts the OT's affirmation that people can actually adequately determine the facts of the matter regarding infractions of the law. Ubiquitous laws punishing various crimes (even to the point of saying, in some cases, that people should not show pity to the condemned) obviously oppose the attitude that punishment and retaliation are intrinsically immoral or barbarous. That God acknowledges the need for vengeance, and promises to provide it himself (Deut. 32:35), confirms this point.

While the Law commands Israelites to love their neighbour and even their enemies, it simultaneously directs them to carry out various kinds of coercion against criminals. It thus does not see any contradiction between the general virtue of seeking the good of the other (love), along with such unqualified commands to love, and using violence in some specifically defined situations (i.e., where the magistrate is delivering justice for the community and God). The objection that violence is "utopian" fails by OT standards because it imputes an intention to the law which the law rejects. That is, it does not use violence out of a sense of utopianism, that simply inflicting state punishment could literally recreate an Edenic paradise. It recognizes that the root cause of crime is the fallen heart of man, and that only the grace of God can solve this problem (Deut. 29:4). The law also commands the Israelites set up judges to render decisions (Deut. 1:9-17), and assumes a family structure of elder rule (Deut. 5:32; 19:12). This demands hierarchy, and contradicts anarchistic reasons for holding to pacifism. Finally, the OT clearly does not require pacifism along divine positive law lines; it rather does the opposite, requiring state punishment by this type of law. Along with the reality of natural law, then, the Old Testament stands opposed to any "natural law" type of argument for pacifism. Conversely, any pacifism which says that the transhistorical "nature of things" requires non-violence would have to teach that the OT was in error. We will return to the significance of this point in section three. However, before getting to Jesus' teachings, we will survey the closest foreground context of his words: the New Testament.

THE NEW TESTAMENT AND PACIFISM

Foreground

The documents of the New Testament provide the earliest foreground for Jesus' teachings, as well as the earliest interpretations of his words. Surveying the corpus of the NT one finds that writers continue to assume as true the background of Jesus' words. To clarify how this is so, the following will recapitulate the four aspects of background the previous section discussed.

Natural Law

The NT assumes and explicitly appeals to natural law in several places. This affirmation of natural law gives us reason to assume that the NT authors would disagree with "moral" pacifism, as the natural law contradicts such a stance, and was known to do so prior to the writing of the NT. It may allow, however, a "divine positive law" or "ceremonial law" pacifism. The burden of proof would be on advocates of pacifism to show that the NT provided such a positive law.

Literary Practices

The context that Dr. Craig Keener noted in regards to Jesus' teaching continued to exist as a background to the NT texts, for the historical era of Jesus' sermon is the same as Paul's epistles, roughly speaking. Thus the NT writers would continue to assume that general rules could be stated with unmentioned exceptions, both in wisdom

21

and in legal contexts. And in fact, they clearly did assume this. For example, Paul could write in 1 Cor. 13:4-7 that:

> Love is patient and kind; love does not envy or boast; it is not arrogant or rude. It does not insist on its own way; it is not irritable or resentful; it does not rejoice at wrongdoing, but rejoices with the truth. Love bears all things, believes all things, hopes all things, endures all things.

Here Paul writes that love "believes all things," which expresses the hermeneutical "principle of charity," the principle that people should be given the benefit of the doubt. Further, he tells us that love is kind in a text that calls Christians to adopt the traits of love. Yet elsewhere he can write in Gal. 5:7-9 and 6:12:

> You were running well. Who hindered you from obeying the truth? This persuasion is not from him who calls you. A little leaven leavens the whole lump. ... It is those who want to make a good showing in the flesh who would force you to be circumcised, and only in order that they may not be persecuted for the cross of Christ.

The apostle clearly regards the Judaizers as untrustworthy and deceivers. Certainly, he does not want the Galatians to "believe all things" these men have been teaching them. And clearly these are not particularly kind sentiments to have towards these individuals. But unless we are to charge Paul with inconsistency here (clearly not a fair charge), we must understand his words in 1 Cor. 13 to have a general applicability, but to allow for exceptions. So the NT provides evidence that it affirms the hermeneutical principles that Dr. Keener mentions.

Social Setting

Paul explicitly confirms that the church was mostly made up of powerless individuals in 1 Cor. 1:20-30:

> Where is the one who is wise? Where is the scribe? Where is the debater of this age? Has not God made foolish the wisdom of the world? For since, in the wisdom of God, the world did not know God through wisdom, it pleased God through the folly of what we preach to save those who believe. For Jews demand signs and Greeks seek wisdom, but we preach Christ crucified, a stumbling block to Jews and folly to Gentiles, but to those who are called, both Jews and Greeks, Christ the power of God and the wisdom of God. For the foolishness of God is wiser than men, and the weakness of God is stronger than men. For consider your calling, brothers: not many of you were wise according to worldly standards, not many were powerful, not many were of noble birth. But God chose what is foolish in the world to shame the wise; God chose what is weak in the world to shame the strong; God chose what is low and despised in the world, even things that are not, to bring to nothing things that are, so that no human being might boast in the presence of God. And because of him you are in Christ Jesus,

23

who became to us wisdom from God, righteousness and sanctification and redemption,
so that, as it is written, "Let the one who
boasts, boast in the Lord.

Paul takes for granted that, in general, the church of
his day is made up of those who are "low and despised in
the world." It is thus natural to assume the apostle would
primarily aim his guidance at this class of people, since
they were his primary audience.

THE NEW TESTAMENT'S USE OF THE OLD TESTAMENT

Providing a definitive explanation of the NT's use of the
OT is of course beyond the scope of a single book,
especially one not directly on the topic. However, we can
argue for a few broadly significant points. Firstly, the
writers of the NT affirm the descriptive authority of the
OT scriptures.[1] Clear examples of this affirmation appear
in Rom. 3:31, 2 Tim. 3:16-17, and 2 Pet. 1:19-21. The first
one is most pertinent for our purposes: "Do we then

---

[1] Bavinck explains the meaning of the term: "[The Protestant churches]
agreed on the premise that Scripture, having God as its author, had
divine authority. This authority was further defined by saying that
Scripture had to be believed and obeyed by everyone and was the only
rule of faith and conduct. This definition, however, automatically led to
a distinction between historical (descriptive) and normative
(prescriptive) authority. Divine revelation, after all, was given in the
form of a history; it has passed through a succession of periods. Far
from everything recorded in Scripture has normative authority for our
faith and conduct. Much of what was commanded and instituted by
God, or prescribed and enjoined by prophets and apostles, no longer
applies to us directly and pertained to persons living in an earlier age"
(Herman Bavinck, *Reformed Dogmatics: Prolegomena* [Grand Rapids: Baker
Academic, 2003], 1:45).

overthrow the law by this faith? By no means! On the contrary, we uphold the law." Ten verses earlier (v. 21), the apostle had written: "But now the righteousness of God has been manifested apart from the law, although the Law and the Prophets bear witness to it." And that text echoes the beginning of the letter, Rom. 1:1-2: "Paul, a servant of Christ Jesus, called to be an apostle of God, set apart for the gospel of God, which he promised beforehand through his prophets in the holy Scriptures...." Rev. Tim Gallant provides the most likely interpretation of 3:31 in his useful work, *These Are Two Covenants: Reconsidering Paul on the Mosaic Law*.

> With regard to 3:31, the most important thing to notice is that already in 3:21, Paul has drawn attention to the distinction between being under Torah, and receiving its witness: "But now apart from Torah the righteousness of God has been revealed, borne witness to by Torah and the prophets." As we have already seen, Paul sometimes plays with *nomos*, alternating the sense of Mosaic covenant and Torah as Scripture. That this is the primary issue in 3:31 is rendered probable by how Paul "establishes the law" in what follows (a point frequently lost because readers give too much weight to chapter breaks). In 4:1, Paul asks, "What therefore shall we say that Abraham our forefather according to the flesh has found?" The entirety of chapter four is an exposition of the narrative portion of Torah, with illustration from a psalm of David: thus, "the law and the prophets" which bear wit-

ness to the righteousness of God (3:21). Consequently, when Paul establishes the law, he is far from securing the continuing validity of the Mosaic covenant. To the contrary, in this very context, he insists that those who are of Torah cannot be heirs of the promise (4:14). Thus, Paul's purpose is to show that the witness of all Scripture has come to full fruition: this is how he establishes the law.[2]

In other words, the apostle affirms the continuing authority of the OT as scripture, though not of Mosaic covenant law as such. Above I argued that Girolamo Zanchi provided the correct rationale for understanding how the NT appeals to the OT on the level of law (not just as scripture, but for directly binding ethical rules). Zanchi asserted:

> How great is the iniquity, then, if Christians want to subject people today, Gentiles and magistrates, to Judaic law? As long as those laws were handed down to the Israelites, they did not apply to the Gentiles. It is only when they coincide with natural law and were confirmed by Christ himself that they apply to all people.[3]

---

[2] Tim Gallant, *These Are Two Covenants: Reconsidering Paul on the Mosaic Law* (2004; Grand Prairie, Alberta: Pactum Reformanda Publishing, 2012), 30-31.

[3] Girolamo Zanchi, *On the Law in General*, Sources in Early Modern Economics, Ethics, and Law, trans. Jeffrey J. Veenstra (Grand Rapids: CLP Academic, 2012), 81.

When we look closely at the discontinuities in rules between the Old and New Testaments, it becomes apparent that the kinds of laws that no longer bind God's people are symbolic and ceremonial in nature: Sabbath laws, kosher laws, the mandate of circumcision, priesthood and temple rules, and the obligation to perform literal sacrifices. In place of these, the NT gives two ceremonial commands: Baptism and Holy Communion. However, the vast majority of NT commands are not of this kind, but are rather expressions of natural law, summed up in the directives to do good, to love, and to act wisely. This has direct relevance for the issue of pacifism, for as we noted above, the overlap between natural law and the OT on the morality of pacifism is complete.

THE APOSTLES ON PACIFISM

Given all these aspects of the NT, we would expect to see them speak in the same way as the OT. And in fact, we do see the apostolic documents contradict the rationales given for "moral pacifism." Once again, these are:

1. The Cycle of violence
2. The Limits of human knowledge
3. The Immorality of punishment and vengefulness
4. The Unloving character of violence
5. The Utopian character of violence
6. Hierarchy as intrinsically dominative

Reasons 1, 2, and 5 (at minimum) directly contradict Paul's words in Rom 13:1-7:

> Let every person be subject to the governing authorities. For there is no authority except

from God, and those that exist have been instituted by God. Therefore whoever resists
the authorities resists what God has appointed, and those who resist will incur judgment.
For rulers are not a terror to good conduct,
but to bad. Would you have no fear of the
one who is in authority? Then do what is
good, and you will receive his approval, for he
is God's servant for your good. But if you do
wrong, be afraid, for he does not bear the
sword in vain. For he is the servant of God,
an avenger who carries out God's wrath on
the wrongdoer. Therefore one must be in
subjection, not only to avoid God's wrath but
also for the sake of conscience. For because
of this you also pay taxes, for the authorities
are ministers of God, attending to this very
thing. Pay to all what is owed to them: taxes
to whom taxes are owed, revenue to whom
revenue is owed, respect to whom respect is
owed, honor to whom honor is owed.

God has appointed governments to enact his vengeance. First, Paul takes for granted that, in fact, those who
resist the government will come to a bad end, and that this
provides them sufficient reason to submit. This means,
however, that a "cycle of violence" argument—suggesting
that government violence will simply provoke equal and
opposite counter-violence, solving nothing—is not a
successful argument. The apostle assumes that government
violence is usually definitive. Second, by assuring
Christians that evildoers will usually suffer for resisting the
government, he assumes that the government will be able

to detect the evildoing. Moreover, since at the time Romans was written unbelievers composed the government, Paul must assume they could determine guilt even without the benefit of the indwelling of the Holy Spirit, regeneration, prophetic gifts, or special grace. Rather, what he likely assumes is that kings do this by means of a gift available to all: wisdom. Shortly after stating that wisdom cries aloud in the streets to the children of men (Prov. 8:1-6), Solomon writes:

> I, wisdom, dwell with prudence, and I find knowledge and discretion. The fear of the Lord is hatred of evil. Pride and arrogance and the way of evil and perverted speech I hate. I have counsel and sound wisdom; I have insight; I have strength. By me kings reign, and rulers decree what is just; by me princes rule, and nobles, all who govern justly. (Prov. 8:12-16)

Thus Paul contradicts the idea that human beings, including unbelieving kings, are incapable of determining the guilt of others. Third, while Paul writes the above about magistrates, he clearly cannot be charged with thinking the state can immanentize the eschaton through its political judgment. No one with common sense living in the real world, as the apostle did, can suggest that human beings with political power can create the New Eden, for they are sinful and fallen just as every other person. And further, since he teaches that God himself has appointed governments to carry out justice, and everywhere contradicts the idea that God intends thereby to usher in the New Creation, Paul cannot possibly be suggesting in this text that political violence will do so. So, assuming Paul was sensible, we must take this passage from Romans to be about a limited, imperfect justice, the only kind of justice a government composed of human beings can ever produce. And this means that Paul denies the premise of reason 5 for pacifism: he teaches that God intends violence to bring in imperfect, but valuable and real, justice, and so contradicts any argument which says using violence must always be accompanied by utopian pretensions.

Other texts eliminate the other rationales for "moral pacifism." Paul describes excommunication, which he (along with Jesus; cf. Matt. 18:15-20) commands churches to perform in various cases (1 Cor. 5:1-13), as "punishment" (Gk. ἐπιτιμία) in 2 Cor. 2:5-8:

> Now if anyone has caused pain, he has caused it not to me, but in some measure—not to put it too severely—to all of you. For such a one, this punishment by the majority is enough, so you should rather turn to forgive and comfort him, or he may be overwhelmed by excessive sorrow. So I beg you to reaffirm your love for him.[4]

It is impossible that Paul would condemn punishment as intrinsically immoral while at the same time commanding Christians to do it. So Paul must also disagree with 3 insofar as it asserts punishment is always wrong. Further, the apostle affirms in Rom. 12:19 the OT teaching that God will take vengeance; this implies, of

---

[4] Paul refers to punishment again in 2 Cor. 7:11.

course, that vengeance *per se* is not wrong. Further still, the NT nowhere condemns the desire for vengeance *per se*; what it rather condemns is "taking" vengeance, which at minimum is an act, not a desire.[5] Yet, we cannot even say that Paul condemns vengeance as an act in itself. Romans 13 clearly rules such a position out by affirming that God himself takes vengeance through the instrument of the state. And a further problem arises for this view when we recognize that vengeance and punishment are not really distinguishable on an essential level. As Thomas Aquinas says (*Summa Theologica* II-II.108.1): "Vengeance consists in the infliction of a penal evil on one who has sinned." In this case "evil" has an ontological, not a moral, significance. It refers to removing a natural good (such as a lack of bodily or emotional pain, or else such as life, or property) from a person as a penalty. So "vengeance" as an act is simply the same thing as enacted punishment. But we have seen that the apostle describes excommunication as a punishment, and he clearly means it, for he recognizes that shunning someone causes them pain (2 Cor. 2:7). Thus we cannot think that Paul means all taking of vengeance is wrong, absolutely speaking. And thus he disagrees with reason 3 for moral pacifism.

The phenomenological differences between state and ecclesiastical punishment may disquiet readers at this point. Are they really similar enough for this defeater argument to be persuasive? For example, unlike state punishment, the Lord and his apostles give direction that

---

[5] Once again, I recommend John Day's book on the imprecatory Psalms, *Crying for Justice*; the fact that the NT approves of the use of imprecations implies it approves of the desire for vengeance in some circumstances.

punishment is to end immediately upon repentance. If the logic of excommunication is purely retributive, surely penitence should be irrelevant. However, things are not so simple. In *The Ways of Judgment*, Dr. Oliver O'Donovan notes a principle relevant to the exercise of punishment:

> Human punishment needs to prove its relation to the preservation of the world. The benefits that flow from retribution are extrinsic only to the bare act of retribution, not extrinsic to its character as judgment. As judgment, punishment is integrated into a web of social and practical practices that serve social and political goods. ... The retributive intuition must be socially situated if we are to claim for it the dignity of an intuition of justice.[6]

He also notes, while commenting on the variety of punishments that various cultures have devised for similar crimes, that "[t]he scale which relates punishments to offenses is inevitably a conventional one."[7] In other words, enacting justice is not done in a vacuum: a correct administration of justice must take into account times and circumstances.

But among the circumstances of all human action, including ecclesiastical action, are all divine laws promulgated by God. Among these laws are Jesus' standing orders for Christians to offer immediate forgiveness to those who repent. Furthermore, this divine law is not accidentally

---

[6] Oliver O'Donovan, *The Ways of Judgment* (Grand Rapids: Eerdmans, 2003), 114-115.

[7] O'Donovan, 120.

related to God's greater purposes in history. And these purposes are ultimately the root of all social and political practices, including the practices of punishment. God desires punishment in this life as a means to an end, that of the preservation of flourishing human society; this is true even for ecclesiastical punishment.[8] Yet that ultimate goal also determines the kinds and frequencies of punishment: if the means to his end were to become destructive to the accomplishment of the end, it would not longer be an effective means.

The nature of ecclesiastical punishment follows from these points. Justice requires that sin be punished, and even in the context of the church, Christ and his apostles have commanded that impenitence and obstinacy in sin be punished by exclusion from the visible church. Yet the general end of the church is to bring glory to God by reconciling people to Jesus through the proclamation of the gospel; the purpose of the church is essentially to spread the mercy of God abroad. Punishment in this community is a kind of accidental necessity, forced upon it by realities of the world, not by its primary purpose. Accordingly, God has decreed that his church not press retributive justice to the point of strict fulfillment in the face of repentance, but to remit all punishments when the hearts of offenders have changed. This is because his purposes in history place a higher value on reconciling

---

[8] This is evident in two ways: 1 Cor. 5:6 requires excommunication for the sake of preserving the character of other church members, and 5:4 requires it so that the Spirit of the Lord will not be so offended by the sin of toleration of known obstinacy that he departs from the visible community. For further argument supporting this latter point, see V. George Shillington, "Atonement Texture in 1 Corinthians," *Journal for the Study of the New Testament* 21 (1999): 29-50.

people into the visible community of the saints than expressing perfect justice through ecclesiastical exclusion. On the other hand, remitting all state punishments on the same principle would quickly lead to societal chaos, contrary to the social order God desires. God's wisdom is on display here, too, for the visible church is not a state but always exists within one, so that it is able to allow the magistrate to worry about staving off chaos through retribution, while it can communicate God's mercy through letting go of ecclesiastical punishment when repentance is forthcoming. For present purposes, this means we can see excommunication as punishment without ignoring the differences its administration has when compared to state punishment.[9]

The practice of excommunication also squarely opposes reason 2, in that it assumes normal Christians are capable of detecting guilt in offending church members. Further, it would seem to contradict reason 1, insofar as the "violence never solves anything" principle bases itself on the natural desire for "getting even" in the human condition. But this desire arises when we are shunned or insulted verbally just as much as it does when we are physically harmed. Yet, nevertheless, Paul commands Christians to excommunicate, to punish, on some occasions. He therefore cannot believe that all punishment

---

[9] Though it should be noted that this difference is not as great as it might appear. Potential wars that fail on the criteria of prospect of success must be abandoned even if there is a just cause; the reason for this is that the higher purpose of the preservation of human society demands mercy be shown to innocent potential victims rather than justice be done to offenders if actors must make the choice between the two. Further, cases of magisterial pardon for crimes flow from the same principles.

inevitably solves nothing. Reasons 4 and 6 remain. NT teaching can easily dispatch the latter. For the NT everywhere contradicts the idea that hierarchies are intrinsically immoral. It does this by affirming hierarchy in the family (e.g., Col. 3:18-25), in the state as we have seen (Rom. 13:1-2), and even in the visible church (e.g., 1 Cor. 16:16; Phil. 1:1; 1 Pet. 5:2; Heb. 13:7, 17; 1 Tim. 2:12-3:7). This leaves only reason 4, that inflicting violence is a violation of the command to love. Yet we have already seen that the OT does not understand the command this way, and that the apostles affirm the truth of the OT. So we have *prima facie* reason to consider the NT as opposed to this logic. Further, we have seen that Paul regards excommunication, an activity the apostle knows to cause harm to the receiver of it, as a good activity in some circumstances; he cannot therefore think that harming someone *per se* is a violation of the command to love, or even the command to love one's enemy. The NT as a whole does not support moral pacifism, and ultimately undermines it. If the NT is supposed to support pacifism, then, the only other way it could do so is via the divine positive law approach.

I will confess at this point that I am unfamiliar with any NT text alleged to support pacifism which also does not seem to express natural moral law. The most commonly cited texts to support pacifism are those that command love, and yet these seem to obviously be moral commands, not merely symbolic or ceremonial ones. And the relative rarity of commands to perform ceremonies in the NT, compared to commands to perform natural duties like love, makes it more likely than not that any given NT command will be an expression of natural law, rather than a *diktat* to perform a symbolic act. There is one possible rationale for a pacifistic symbolic practice that can be ruled out, though. The NT affirms that there needs to be both magistrates punishing people in the *polis*, and communities punishing their members in the *ekklesia*. Whatever else this means, it forces the readers of the NT to recognize that the present Age is not a total reversion to Eden. Unlike the original state, the present age contains sin, and requires retributive response from human beings. Thus, there can be no positive law rationale for pacifism that presupposes the present age is exactly like the original, sinless state, for it is not. It is unlike Eden both in the presence of sin, and in the assumption that punitive acts, acts which harm others by definition, are good and necessary things.

This brings us to the end of our general survey of the NT. We have now shown that the background context of Jesus' teaching, and the immediate foreground, which provides the earliest interpretation of Jesus' words, do not express pacifism. Rather, the natural conclusion to draw from both sets of data is wholly in line with a magisterial Protestant approach to violence, personal virtue, and the state. This provides strong *prima facie* grounds to assume Jesus did not mean to teach pacifism, whatever he did mean. Yet, it would be inappropriate to conclude the argument at this point. A positive explanation of what Jesus did mean cannot be avoided, for two main reasons. First, because Jesus' own explicit teaching can hardly be avoided in answering the question of his position on violence. Second, because of all places in scripture, advocates of pacifism have pointed to Jesus' commands as the source of their position, often interpreting them as divine positive law requiring such a practice. Thus, the next section will take up the challenge of answering this argument.

III:

THE TEACHINGS OF CHRIST

AT LAST we come to the matter at hand, and answer the question: was Jesus a pacifist? The previous sections in this book have provided strong *prima facie* evidence from Jesus' background context and the earliest foreground interpretation of his legacy, that he was not a pacifist. Now a positive explication of Jesus' teaching and example are needed.

The strongest and most common arguments for pacifism from Jesus' teaching come from a few places in the Gospels. Primarily, these seem to be: the temptation narrative, the Sermon the Mount (and parallel texts), his teaching about taking up the cross, his teaching about Caesar, his teaching about Gentile rulers, and his teaching about taking the sword. Another argument comes from Jesus' acceptance of his own crucifixion.

REFUSING SATAN'S TEMPTATION

In Matthew's account, the final temptation given to Jesus is world domination (Matt. 4:8-11):

> Again, the devil took him to a very high
> mountain and showed him all the kingdoms

of the world and their glory. And he said to him, "All these I will give you, if you will fall down and worship me." Then Jesus said to him, "Be gone, Satan! For it is written, "'You shall worship the Lord your God and him only shall you serve.'" Then the devil left him, and behold, angels came and were ministering to him.

The pacifistic argument from this account usually follows the logic that this temptation represents the "zealot option" for Jesus' ministry, and that in rejecting it, Jesus rejects violence *in toto*. However, there are several reasons to reject this interpretation. First, it wrongly conflates a zealot ideology, which is really a Holy War option, with a just war approach. Just war thinking follows certain criteria, including: (a) that a legitimate authority must wage war, (b) that the prospects of success in war must be probable for waging it to be licit, and (c) that acts of war should discriminate between the guilty and the innocent. Holy war thinking need not follow any of these criteria, and often has not in history.

Second, it overlooks the background to these temptations. In the wilderness temptation, Jesus recapitulates Israel's wilderness wandering, but succeeds where Israel failed. This point is highlighted in the mode of Jesus' reply: he quotes the word of God as sufficient reason for his obedience to God. He obeys God's commands where Israel failed. In the desert, Israel caved into the temptation to worship idols. So in the present temptation, the command Jesus cites in reply to Satan is not "You shall not kill", but "You shall worship the Lord your God, and him only shall you serve."

A good positive explanation of this text is provided by the demonology of the NT. Paul teaches in 1 Cor. 10:20 that: "what pagans sacrifice they offer to demons and not to God. I do not want you to be participants with demons." Further, the apostle confirms this assessment of Satan in a sense, when he states that the devil is (2 Cor. 4:4) "the god of this world", and the apostle John echoes this concept in his first epistle (1 John 5:19): "the whole world lies in the power of the evil one." For the NT, to live in any way other than obedience to God is, *de facto*, to be subject to and in fellowship with demons. Fellowship with evil can give pleasures for a time, including the pleasures of power. This is the temptation Jesus faced, and it is in fact the ultimate temptation: the temptation to replace God with the creature in our moral universe. Jesus' rejection goes much deeper than a refusal of a certain kind of political tactic; his reply goes to the heart of the problem with the human condition. And this leads to the second background to the text, which is the failure of humanity at its origin, the fall of Adam and Eve in the garden. And what was the temptation they faced? Not the temptation to use violence, but the temptation to distrust God, and to strive for their desires in disobedience to his commands. It is this fundamental problem that Jesus' refusal to worship Satan addresses, and not an ethically downstream matter like zealot violence.

THE SERMON ON THE MOUNT

In the preface to his book, *The Sermon on the Mount: Inspiring the Moral Imagination*, Dr. Dale C. Allison writes about two common errors in exegesis of this sermon:

Some people would say that the Sermon on the Mount is the quintessence of Christianity. I am not among them. The erroneous conviction comes from the unfortunate habit of viewing the Sermon in isolation. Readers, especially modern readers, have again and again interpreted Matthew 5-7 as though the chapters were complete unto themselves, as though they constituted a book rather than a portion of a book. Symptomatic is the occasional reprinting of the Sermon in anthologies of literature. But the three chapters that constitute the Sermon on the Mount, chapters surrounded on either side by twenty-five additional chapters, neither summarize the rest of Matthew nor sum up adequately the faith of Jesus, much less the religion of our evangelist. How could anything that fails to refer explicitly to the crucifixion and resurrection be the quintessence of Matthew's Christian faith? Here context is everything. Any credible interpretation of Matthew 5-7 must constantly keep an eye on Matthew 1-4 and Matthew 9-28. For the part (the Sermon) loses its meaning apart from the whole (Matthew's Gospel). The Sermon on the Mount is in the middle of a story, and it is the first goal of this little commentary to interpret the discourse accordingly.

There is a second way in which this commentary seeks to place the Sermon in context. All too often in the past–the strategy goes all the way back to Tertullian and Augustine–the Sermon has been read against Judaism. That is, the superiority of Jesus and the church over against Judaism has been promoted by arguing that this word of Jesus or that expression of Matthew brings us, within the world of first-century Judaism, something startlingly new, or even impossible. Most such claims, however, do not stand up under scrutiny. What we rather have in the Sermon is the product of a messianic Judaism; and, as we know from the writings of Friedlander (1911), Abrahams (1917, 1924), and Montefiore (1927, 1930), most of the sentiments found in the Sermon already appear, at least here or there, in old Jewish sources. It is primarily the relationship of those sentiments to one another and, above all, their relationship to the person of Jesus and his story that gives them their unique meaning for Christians. So responsible exegesis will seek to highlight the continuity between the Sermon and Jewish teaching, whether within the Hebrew Bible or without, and moreover the immense debt of the former to the latter. The time of polemic against Judaism is over. So too is the time when Christians could pretend, in the words of Adolf Harnack, to find in the Sermon on the Mount teaching "freed from all external and particularistic features."[1]

---

[1] Dale C. Allison, *The Sermon on the Mount* (New York: Crossroad, 1999),

The following commentary on Jesus' teaching will attempt to do what Dr. Allison suggests should be done, i.e. interpret the sermon in these two contexts. In many cases, I will simply be following Dr. Allison's lead in doing so. Dr. Allison also highlights another important aspect of this sermon that some interpreters throughout the centuries have missed:

> One must reckon seriously with the fact that the Sermon on the Mount is partly a poetic text. By this is meant that it is, unlike codes of law, dramatic and pictorial. The reader sees a man offering a sacrifice in Jerusalem (5:23), someone in prison (5:25-26), a body without eye and hand (5:29-30), someone being slapped (5:39), the sun rising (5:45), the rain falling (5:45), someone praying in a closet (6:6), lilies in a field (6:28), a log in an eye (7:4), wolves in sheeps' clothing (7:15). These images and comments upon the sermon hardly add up to anything can be called legislation. The Sermon does not offer a set of rules—the ruling on divorce is the exception[2]—but rather seeks to instill a moral vision. ...

---

xi-xii.

[2] Dr. Craig Keener argues that this is not a true exception to the wisdom genre of the rest of the Sermon:

> Many of the sayings in Jesus' sermon on divine law in Matthew 5:21-28 may have originally been spoken in non-legal contexts, but if *any* of the "antitheses" has an originally legal force, it must be this prohibition of divorce. Most of the other prohibitions—anger, lust, swearing, and hatred of enemies—are difficult for a court to detect, much less enforce. But divorce, like the prohibi-

The Sermon's primary purpose is to instill principles and qualities through a vivid inspiration of the moral imagination. What one comes away with is not a grossly incomplete set of statutes but an unjaded impression of a challenging moral ideal.[3]

---

tion against legal retaliation, *could* (though need not) involve a Jewish court in its action, if only to issue a certificate of divorce. The prohibition against swearing would involve a court official only if someone needed a rabbi to dissolve an invalid vow.

But the context of the divorce saying suggests we take it more in line with the others here: a combination of a wisdom saying and a prophetic summons, whose sanctions were guaranteed by the apocalyptic judgment of the heavenly court. (*And Marries Another*, 23)

Dr. Keener continues his explanation, after noting Matthew probably added it to the original dominical saying without it:

But in Matthew, where the rule appears in the context of the exposition of Scripture and where there is an emphasis on the church disciplining erring members, the rule is more likely to be *applied* in a legal way. That is why it is significant that in Matthew the saying is qualified: "except in the case of immorality."

Why would Matthew insist on such an exception? Precisely because Jesus' teaching on divorce, like most of his other teachings, is not detailed legal formulation like those of some other teachers of his day. He emphasized finding *principles* in the law, viewing God's Word as prophetic demand rather than merely case law demanding legal extrapolation. If Jesus' words were to become legal formulations in any sense, they would have to be qualified as legal formulations are. And if Jesus' words were not to become a *mere* legal formulation, the real principle inherent in those words must be preserved *against* a legalistic interpretation of those words. (*And Marries Another*, 26, 27)

[3] Allison, *Sermon on the Mount*, 11.

Below, we will highlight the texts used most often to support pacifism in order to show how they do not, as well as various other aspects of the Sermon that confirm Allison's general analysis.

As a final prefatory note, Dr. Allison views the sermon as chiastically structured:

A. Introduction (5:1-2)

    B. Blessings (5:3-12)

        C Law and Prophets (5:17-20)

            D Jesus and Torah (two triads) (5:21-48)

                E Almsgiving, Prayer, Fasting (6:1-4)

            D' Social issues (two triads) (6:19-7:11)

        C' Law and Prophets (7:12)

    B' Warnings (7:13-27)

A' Conclusion (7:28-8:1)[4]

Beatitudes

Dr. Allison notes the extensive Isaianic background to the Sermon and its explication elsewhere in the Gospel. This begins with the Beatitudes, which echo the Prophet in various ways:

> "Blessed are those who mourn, for they will be comforted" borrows from Isa. 61:2. "Blessed are the poor in spirit, for theirs is the kingdom of God" is inspired by Isa. 61:1. And "Rejoice and be glad" recalls Isa 61:10 ("I will greatly rejoice in the Lord, and my whole being exult in my God").[5]

---

[4] Allison, *Sermon on the Mount*, 36.

[5] Allison, *Sermon on the Mount*, 15.

As Dr. Allison notes, this dependence on Isaiah has significance for interpretation of the Sermon:

> It means above all that the authority who speaks the Sermon belongs to a history. Jesus is not an isolated novum on humanity's religious landscape. He is rather the goal of a story, the history told in the Jewish Bible. To say that Jesus is the anointed one prophesied by Isaiah 61 is to say that he has been sent by the same God who spoke to Abraham, Moses, David, and the prophets; it is to imply that there is continuity between the new and the old and that ultimately the one who speaks here through his anointed prophet is the one whose words and deeds constitute the religious story of Israel.
>
> That this is indeed the case is confirmed by 5:17-20. Sometimes religions begin when a charismatic figure overthrows the traditions of the past. Buddha, for instance, appeared and rejected the Hinduism of his time and place. But Jesus does not reject his religious tradition; he is rather a reformer of it. He comes not to abolish the law and the prophets, whose imperatives remain in force. The God who spoke then speaks again now, in the Sermon. And he does not contradict himself.[6]

The most directly relevant beatitude to the issue of pacifism is obviously 5:9: blessed are the peacemakers, for

---

[6] Allison, *Sermon on the Mount*, 16-17.

they will be called the sons of God. This beatitude says nothing that is not expressed or implied in several OT texts, including: Ps. 34:14; 37:35-38; 120:1-7; and Prov. 12:20. These texts are part of a non-pacifist corpus and era of redemptive history, and so cannot be interpreted in a pacifistic manner. However, they can be interpreted in other ways. First, the virtue of seeking for peace is eminently useful and good in personal relations. Second, even in the matter of statecraft, the just war tradition has always emphasized war should be the last resort taken. So there is both personal and political expression to the virtue of peacemaking.

Salt and Light

The words about salt and light give the first of the actual commands of the Sermon, but they do not explain how people are to carry them out. Dr. Allison explains that "the sayings" about salt and light "together constitute a transitional passage that functions as a general heading for 5:17-7:12, where those issues are addressed. Matt. 5:13-16 moves readers from the life of the blessed future (depicted in 5:3-12) to the demands of the present, and so the theme switches from gift to task."[7]

JESUS, THE LAW, AND THE PROPHETS

At this point we must return to Dr. Allison's structural analysis above, which points out the bracketing of the sermon with references to continuity of Jesus' teaching with the Law and the Prophets (5:17-20 and 7:12). This primes us to read the Sermon in continuity with the OT,

---

[7] Allison, *Sermon on the Mount*, 31.

and given what the OT background says about the premises of pacifism, this is not good news for the pacifistic position.

The various components of 5:17-20 deserve particular attention. Dr. R.T. France explains the meaning of the words "Do not think that I have come to abolish the Law or the Prophets":

> "Do not suppose ..." might be no more than a teaching device to draw attention to Jesus' positive statement by first setting out its opposite (cf. 10:34), but it is not unlikely that there were in fact some who did suppose that Jesus was against the law and the prophets. His disagreements with the scribes over the correct way to observe the law (notably with regard to the sabbath, see 12:1–14) would easily have given them the impression that he sat light to the authority of the law itself; the same charge persisted with regard to his followers (Acts 6:11, 13–14; 21:28). By the time Matthew was writing, the "freedom from the law" message of some of Christianity's leading teachers would have strengthened this impression. Jesus, it seemed, had set himself up against the written word of God. The issue is not simply an accusation of failing to keep the law in practice, but of aiming to "abolish" scriptural authority. The verb *katalyō* is used of dismantling and destroying a building or institution (24:2; 26:61; 27:40); with reference to an authoritative text it means to declare that it is no longer valid, to repeal or annul.

> The issue is thus not Jesus' personal practice
> as such, but his attitude to the authority of the
> law and the prophets.[8]

Jesus, then, directly denies he has come to annul the authority of scripture. Any interpretation of his teachings in the Sermon that implies he has done so, pits Jesus against himself, and should be a last resort for any charitable interpreter.

On the meaning of "but to fulfill" in v. 17, Dr. Allison once again provides the most likely interpretation, that of fulfill as "eschatologically fulfills the prophecies of the OT":

> Matthew usually uses the verb in question
> ("fulfill") with reference to prophetic fulfill-
> ment (1:22; 4:14; 12:17; etc.) and because our
> sentence refers not just to the Law but also to
> the Prophets. So Jesus' new teaching brings to
> realization that which the Torah prophesied.
> And that realization does not set the Law and
> Prophets aside. Fulfillment rather confirms
> the Torah's truth.[9]

Yet, this interpretation lacks completeness without an explanation of its relevance to the ethical teaching that follows in the Sermon. Dr. Greg Welty provides the best solution to this problem:

---

[8] R.T. France, *The Gospel of Matthew*, New International Commentary on the New Testament (Grand Rapids: Eerdmans, 2007), 181-82.

[9] Allison, *Sermon on the Mount*, 59.

Why do I say this? Well, it is precisely because the entirety of OT revelation, that seamless fabric of the law and the prophets, consistently prophesy a coming Saviour from sin, that we would expect the Saviour pictured by that revelation to confirm those Mosaic laws which the Pharisees subjected to distortion. For the same Christ whose life is the ground of our imputed righteousness, is the Christ whose life is the pattern for our practical righteousness, our Christian sanctification. Since throughout the NT, one and the same life of Christ is both the grounds of our righteousness (his obedience to God's moral law) and the pattern for our righteousness (his example to us), we would never expect Christ to drive a wedge between the moral law to which he submitted (OT moral law), and the practical righteousness he commended to his followers (via his own life and ethical teaching). The eschatological *pleroô* of v. 17, by which Jesus declares that he really is that Saviour from sin promised on every page of the OT, only reinforces this point.[10]

Dr. Welty notes that the connecting word of v. 19 (οὖν, "therefore") entails that the responsibility to obey OT law follows from Jesus' coming to fulfill the law (a point which 17-18 elaborates upon). Verse 20's linking word, "for" (γάρ) "reminds us that the kingdom righteousness exemplified in Jesus' teaching, is not merely

---

[10] Welty, "Eschatological Fulfilment."

distinctive to the inhabitants of the kingdom of heaven; it is a condition of entry into the kingdom of heaven ('you will by no means enter')!"[11]

The Isaianic background to the Sermon noted above provides further support for Welty's argument. For Isaiah depicts a future for the Law, with two aspects. Firstly in Isa. 21:1-4:

> It shall come to pass in the latter days
> that the mountain of the house of the Lord
> shall be established as the highest of the mountains,
> and shall be lifted up above the hills;
> and all the nations shall flow to it,
> and many peoples shall come, and say:
> "Come, let us go up to the mountain of the Lord,
> to the house of the God of Jacob,
> that he may teach us his ways
> and that we may walk in his paths."
> For out of Zion shall go the law,
> and the word of the Lord from Jerusalem.
> He shall judge between the nations,
> and shall decide disputes for many peoples;
> and they shall beat their swords into plowshares,
> and their spears into pruning hooks;
> nation shall not lift up sword against nation,
> neither shall they learn war anymore.

---

[11] Welty, "Eschatological Fulfilment."

The Law shall go forth and discipline the rule the nations. Yet at the same time, in the future, God will not treat some individuals exactly the same as he did in the Mosaic system (Isa. 56:3-5):

> Let not the foreigner who has joined himself
> to the Lord say,
> "The Lord will surely separate me from his
> people";
> and let not the eunuch say,
> "Behold, I am a dry tree."
> For thus says the Lord:
> "To the eunuchs who keep my Sabbaths,
> who choose the things that please me
> and hold fast my covenant,
> I will give in my house and within my walls
> a monument and a name
> better than sons and daughters;
> I will give them an everlasting name
> that shall not be cut off.

Such a practice would contradict Deut. 23:1-8. How can the continuity and discontinuity of the Law in Isaiah's vision of the future be understood?

The tension can be resolved if we recognize that Isaiah stresses the continuity of the law on a matter where it is in continuity with the created order (i.e., natural law), that is, where the law teaches people to good to one another and live at peace. On the other hand, he stresses discontinuity on ceremonial and cultic matters, where God instilled divisions between people in order to symbolize and signify various realities to the Israelites. In the future, Isaiah suggests, these symbolic laws will no longer be in effect. Rather, the reality to which they point as an entire system of symbols, the restoration of human nature and the reconciliation of the human race, will come into being, and thus these symbolic laws will no longer be necessary.

As we will see below, this interpretation of Isaiah perfectly explains the logic of the connection between Matt. 5:17's "fulfill" and the rest of the Sermon on the Mount. First, however, we must note that immediate context of this word, vs. 18-19, and elaborate on the meaning of "fulfill":

> For truly, I say to you, until heaven and earth pass away, not an iota, not a dot, will pass from the Law until all is accomplished. Therefore whoever relaxes one of the least of these commandments and teaches others to do the same will be called least in the kingdom of heaven, but whoever does them and teaches them will be called great in the kingdom of heaven.

The connecting γάρ at the beginning of v. 18 provides a further reason for v. 17's statement. Jesus' teaching here echoes rabbinic Jewish statements that affirm the absolute and unchangeable authority of the scriptures, as Dr. Craig Keener has noted:

> He announces in v. 18 that the law will stand until the time when heaven and earth pass away– in other words, until the end of the world (cf. 24:35). Most Jewish readers understood this as a figure of speech meaning that the law would stand "forever," a suggestion of the eternality of the covenant. Jesus cer-

tainly understands the law to be eternal; its sanctions are executed at the day of judgment (5:19-20).

Indeed, as v. 18 continues, not one yod (the smallest Hebrew letter) or marking was to pass from the law. ... [E]ven the least noticed parts of God's Word are eternally true and valid. Later Jewish teachers often spoke in similar ways about the importance of even the most trivial elements: they spoke of how God would rather uproot a thousand king Solomons than a single yod from the Bible; or they told how a yod removed from Sarai's name in Genesis cried out to God from generation to generation, until he finally stuck it back into the Bible, in Joshua's name. Although there is no way to know how early these Jewish stories are, they at least illustrate the point that Jesus' readers would have no doubt understood: he was upholding the veracity of even the smallest details of God's Word.[12]

On verse 19, Dr. Keener writes:

When Jesus condemns breaking even the smallest of commandments, he is espousing an idea that most of his hearers would have readily understood. By the third century many rabbis had even decided which commandment was the lightest and which was the heaviest....The rabbis thereby affirmed that

---

[12] Keener, 114-115.

one who performed a single precept was regarded as if he had kept the whole law, and one suspected of violating one precept could easily be suspected of violating any other. Indeed, a Jew could not become a Pharisee, and a Gentile could not convert to Judaism if he were unwilling to keep even a single, little-known law. As one scholar points out, "Deliberate rejection of any commandment was, in the later rabbinic formulation, tantamount to rejecting the God who gave it."

The point is not that no one ever breaks a commandment; the rabbis admitted that virtually everyone breaks some commandments sometimes. The point is that no one has the right to say, "I like these commandments over here, but those little commandments over there are not worth my attention." To deny that one was responsible to do whatever God commanded, no matter how trivial it may seem, was to deny his lordship and to intentionally rebel against his whole law. According to the rabbis, such a person merited damnation.[13]

Verse 19 continues the logical flow of Jesus' teaching, drawing a consequence from the inviolable authority of the divine word. That is, verse 18 and 19 work like this: because the scriptures are the word of God, they cannot be contradicted by the course of history. And because of that same characteristic, i.e. the divine authority of the

---

[13] Keener, 116-117.

scriptures, no one can rightly alter the law in their exposition of its demands.

Of course, a problem arises for many at this point. For a cursory glance at the rest of the NT shows many cases where OT laws are clearly no longer binding for Christians. As we saw earlier, these cases are: Sabbath, food, priesthood and temple, circumcision, and sacrificial laws. The common feature of these laws provides the solution, however. All of these laws are ceremonial and symbolic, and are not mere expressions of natural law, like the teaching of the rest of the Sermon. And this is precisely in accord with the eschatological vision of the OT, seen even in Isaiah as we explained above. For in the *eschaton* envisioned in the law and the prophets, natural law (the created order) would be obeyed, but the ceremonial divisions and restrictions on humanity, intended to symbolize the problem with creation (sin and its effects) and the solution to that problem (judgment and restoration), would no longer be in effect, the reality to which they pointed having already come. This is the logic that explains Jesus' consistency with the rest of the NT. Jesus' elaboration on this point throughout the rest of the Sermon provides commands and directions in full continuity with the OT; in none of the cases does he uphold as still in effect the ceremonial laws elsewhere abrogated.[14] Rather, he upholds the law as binding

---

[14] Arguably the teaching about sacrifice 5:23-24 contradicts this point, but once we recognize that Jesus simply took this an example from the historical context of his original audience, which at that time were living prior to the crucifixion and its redemptive-historical consequences, the problem evaporates, for natural law itself directs us to obey it in light of specific circumstances, and all the best observers of natural law have always noted this aspect of its force for us.

precisely in the places where it expresses the abiding norms of the created order, or the natural law.

The last verse of this introductory passage is v. 20, and here again Dr. Welty provides the best exegesis: "v. 20 gives a single, unifying theme to vv. 21-48: it is the righteousness of the scribes and Pharisees which is being exposed as fraudulent and in need of correction, not the OT." Indeed, this theme extends beyond verse 48 and into chapters 6-7. In the rest of the sermon, Jesus constantly contrasts the true righteousness the kingdom demands with the hypocrisy and unrighteousness of the Pharisees. Contrary to some interpreters, who have attempted to defend a view of the Sermon as surpassing the demands of the Law by arguing the Pharisees were examples of perfect obedience to the Law, Jesus is quite clear of his view of Pharisaical righteousness (Matt. 23:23, 27-28):

> Woe to you, scribes and Pharisees, hypocrites! For you tithe mint and dill and cumin, and have neglected the weightier matters of the law: justice and mercy and faithfulness. These you ought to have done, without neglecting the others. …
>
> Woe to you, scribes and Pharisees, hypocrites! For you are like whitewashed tombs, which outwardly appear beautiful, but within are full of dead people's bones and all uncleanness. So you also outwardly appear righteous to others, but within you are full of hypocrisy and lawlessness.

Jesus' demand in 5:20, then, is not about "surpassing the demands of the Law," but about truly obeying it, in contrast to the Pharisees who merely pretend to, while being truly lawless.

The consequence of this analysis must be, at minimum, to incline interpreters to seek for continuity between the OT and the Sermon in the 5:21-48.

RETALIATION AND LOVE YOUR ENEMIES

The most important aspect of the Sermon for the subject of pacifism is 5:38-48

> "You have heard that it was said, 'An eye for an eye and a tooth for a tooth.' But I say to you, Do not resist the one who is evil. But if anyone slaps you on the right cheek, turn to him the other also. And if anyone would sue you and take your tunic, let him have your cloak as well. And if anyone forces you to go one mile, go with him two miles. Give to the one who begs from you, and do not refuse the one who would borrow from you.
>
> "You have heard that it was said, 'You shall love your neighbor and hate your enemy.' But I say to you, Love your enemies and pray for those who persecute you, so that you may be sons of your Father who is in heaven. For he makes his sun rise on the evil and on the good, and sends rain on the just and on the unjust. For if you love those who love you, what reward do you have? Do not even the tax collectors do the same? And if you greet only your brothers, what more are you doing than others? Do not even the Gentiles

> do the same? You therefore must be perfect,
> as your heavenly Father is perfect."

We have already argued that not taking vengeance, and instead doing good to one's enemies, was commanded in the OT and the rest of the NT, and that in the OT specifically, it is quite clear such commands were consistent with participation in state violence. However, some positive interpretation of this text is needed. And while it may seem banal, we should take care to note that in none of the examples Jesus gives of obeying the command, does he describe a magistrate specifically. All of the examples are drawn from the normal life of an average, politically powerless, Israelite. This should incline us to affirm the old Augustinian interpretation of these texts, that they are talking about interpersonal conflict in the private realm, not the public role of the magistrate.

Further, the implication of Jesus' choice of examples in the first antithesis is that he has in mind a particular interpretation of the *lex talionis*, not the law *per se*, as his opponent. It is the application of the law to private life, in a way that justifies taking private vengeance, precisely the course of action the OT prohibits. In the second antithesis, regarding love of enemy, scholars have long noted that no such command as "hate your enemy" ever appears in the OT, and this is true. As we argued, the OT commands love of enemy. This is not true, however, for all Jewish tradition, where one can find explicit commands not to do good to evil people.[15] It is certainly these Jewish

---

[15] Dr. Kenneth Bailey pointed out one such example in Sirach 12:1-7, which concludes (NRSV): "Give to the one who is good, but do not help the sinner." Dr. Bailey comments: "Thus, help offered to sinners may be labor against God Himself who detests sinners. Furthermore,

traditions, and not the OT scriptures, which Jesus is correcting here, by reiterating OT ethics.

TAKING UP THE CROSS

Another command pacifists will sometimes appeal to is Jesus' "take up your cross, and follow me" (Matt. 16:24). Dr. Yoder argued that this command was essentially a command to be a faithful minority community under persecution.[16] However, as some have noted in response to Dr. Yoder's work,[17] at times he can seem to reduce the

---

sinners' hands should not be strengthened. Clearly Ben Sirach cautions against helping *any* stranger." Kenneth E. Bailey, *Poet & Peasant and Through Peasant Eyes: A Literary-Cultural Approach to the Parables of Luke* (Grand Rapids: Eerdmans, 1983), 44.

[16] John Howard Yoder, *The Original Revolution: Essays on Christian Pacifism* (Waterloo, Ontario: Herald Press, 2003), 32, and *The Politics of Jesus* (Grand Rapids: Eerdmans, 1972), 124-125.

[17] Mennonite theologian Dr. Stephen F. Lintaman writes: "This marginalizing of human subjectivity or of the personal meaning of faith is clearly and cleverly stated in Yoder's *The Original Revolution*. Yoder discusses "the Bultmanns and the Grahams" and "the Peales and Robertses" of this world who stress the personal, inward meaning of the Gospel. He agrees that the Gospel speaks to personal questions of anxiety and guilt and lack of meaning in life, but his point is that this personal meaning is only secondary-only accidental-to the real Gospel message itself:

> Neo-Anabaptist readings of the Gospel and the human condition do lay bare our bondage to the great social powers of nationalism and materialism. But they do not penetrate into the insecurities, anxieties and shame of the human spirit which make these idols so attractive and powerful in the first place. Hence neo-Anabaptism could not show real compassion for the weak and give a sympathetic account of human idolatry, nor could it speak clearly of the spiritual power that can deliver men and women from bondage into the kingdom of freedom. Neo-Anabaptism called for a far-reaching conversion that required something as basic and fundamental

meaning of the Gospel to politics, and this problem becomes evident here. In Luke 9 and 14 we find parallel versions of this command, and I will begin my analysis with them. In Luke 9:23-25 we read:

> And He was saying to them all, "If anyone wishes to come after Me, he must deny himself, and take up his cross daily and follow Me. For whoever wishes to save his life will lose it, but whoever loses his life for My sake, he is the one who will save it. For what is a man profited if he gains the whole world, and loses or forfeits himself?

And later in chapter 14:26-27, 33 we see:

> If anyone comes to Me, and does not hate his own father and mother and wife and children and brothers and sisters, yes, and even his own life, he cannot be My disciple. Whoever does not carry his own cross and come after Me cannot be My disciple. ... So then, none of you can be My disciple who does not give up all his own possessions.

---

and *personal* as a complete change of human allegiance. Yet somehow that change was to be made without a gospel that was addressed to the personal, subjective side of human existence. Deciding against the kingdom of evil and for the kingdom of Christ was apparently an objective intellectual decision that took clear insight and a firm will but not a healed or liberated heart. ("The Pastoral Significance of the Anabaptist Vision", in *Refocusing a Vision: Shaping Anabaptist Character in the 21st Century*, [Goshen, IN: Mennonite Historical Society, 1995] https://www.goshen.edu/mhl/Refocusing/ DINTAMAN.htm [accessed September 30, 2016]).

What does Jesus mean by this command? We can begin by noting what carrying a cross implied. The cross was an instrument by which the Romans would kill you, and if you were carrying it, it meant you were about to die. This brings us to the first qualification in the command: Luke says any would-be disciples must carry the cross every day. But of course, the Romans would not be making you do this every day, if they were literally making you do it. You would make that journey only once.

The second qualification comes from the near historical context of the command. It is clear that Jesus did not literally mean all true disciples would die from public execution. The closing narrative of the Gospel of John (the end of chapter 21), for example, seems to deny this. It replies to a misunderstanding about the death of the beloved disciple, wherein some early Christians had thought the disciple would not die. The Gospel clarifies that Jesus did not promise this; but it does so by saying the issue was really none of the church's concern. It does not suggest that the survival of the beloved disciple would be impossible because all Christians must die from state persecution. And it is ultimately statistically impossible that, in the first generation of the church, no Christians died except by state persecution. Even one elderly convert who passed away by natural causes would disprove such an interpretation of Jesus' words. So whatever application Jesus' words have, we can see at least two reasons why it must be broader than such a woodenly literal interpretation. On a *prima facie* level, the "daily" requirement would more naturally seem to mean that He is asking them to be *willing* to carry the cross any day, if necessary.

Another part of Jesus' intellectual context can help us to understand what could be included in the "cross" he speaks about. While Dr. Yoder is correct to note the cross can be a symbol of state persecution, the early church also believed that they could be persecuted by demons. The most obvious example of this is demonization, but the wider nature of this demonic threat also appears in passages like Heb. 2:14-15:

> Since therefore the children share in flesh and blood, he himself likewise partook of the same things, that through death he might destroy the one who has the power of death, that is, the devil, and deliver all those who through fear of death were subject to lifelong slavery.

Proximately, Satan has power over death in this world. All death is in some sense a Satanic event, though ultimately it is also derived from God's curse (about which, see more below). This fear of death binds people to slavery, in an attempt to assuage their fears and palliate them with sinful pleasures. It is precisely this bondage that Christ frees people from, as the passage goes on to say (2:17-18):

> Therefore he had to be made like his brothers in every respect, so that he might become a merciful and faithful high priest in the service of God, to make propitiation for the sins of the people. For because he himself has suffered when tempted, he is able to help those who are being tempted.

Christ defeated the ultimate persecutor, Satan, by showing the way through death, thus eliminating the threat sensed within death, and thereby eliminating the fear it produces and the bondage that comes from that fear. This redemptive work was for everyone, and it applies to the fear of death that all people face. And yet we know that there are more ways to die in life than by means of state persecution. Satan has more than one tool in his kit. There is no reason to think state persecution is the only kind of demonic harassment Christians might face.

Returning to Jesus' own words, we can gain greater understanding of his meaning through some of the contrasts with obedience that he mentions. Carrying the cross is set in opposition to some other possible choices. Among them are not hating one's family, and not giving up all of one's possessions. In one of his rhetorical questions, he even raises the possibility of actions that would gain someone "the whole world". Yet, even within the Gospels there are examples of people with families and possessions following Jesus. Further, Jesus reiterates the command to honour one's mother and father to the rich young ruler (Mark 10:17-27). This again means that we must qualify Jesus' statements. Earlier we noted that the command to carry the cross meant more literally a command to be willing to do so. Now we can add that the Lord is not commanding his disciples to give up goods and kindred for no reason, but rather to do so only if necessity imposes upon them the choice between those created realities and the Lord.

Jesus also contrasts another set of behaviours with carrying the cross. They are saving one's own life, and not denying oneself. It is easy to see that these are the essential opposite to carrying the cross. Carrying the cross means being willing to die; refusal to carry the cross is rooted in not being so willing. And, given the nature of the universe, to be willing to die is to be willing to give up contact with every good thing in it, so that in effect, to be willing to carry the cross is to be willing to give up everything in the world.

In sum, this command requires nothing more of us than the Greatest Commandment does. To be commanded to serve God with everything one has, means being willing to obey him even to the point of death, if the only alternative is to disobey him. Insofar as Jesus claims to be the Lord himself, the Greatest Command would require us to carry our cross.

And this was not merely a teaching on this part; Jesus practiced what he preached here. The cross was of course the means by which the Lord himself would choose to lay down his life in order to obey his Father. When, in the Garden of Gethsemane, Jesus asked if another way was possible, he nevertheless concluded that he would accept the way of the cross if it were necessary in the providential will of the Father. When the Lord commands us not just to pick up a cross, but to follow him while doing so, we can see what he means. He calls us to make the exact same choice he did: to accept death from the hands of God if providence gives us no choice between it and sin. It means, in essence, to be willing to give up everything and to endure anything rather than disobey God. His command goes to the very heart of the problem with the human condition. From the first sin, human beings have been choosing sin for the sake of some lesser good rather than obedience to their Creator. Jesus calls us to finally do what we were made to do, to serve God above all things.

One of Jesus' earliest interpreters confirms this understanding of what he means. When Paul takes up this same theme of following the pattern of the death of Christ, he applies the concept in much the same way (2 Cor. 4:5-18):

> For what we proclaim is not ourselves, but Jesus Christ as Lord, with ourselves as your servants for Jesus' sake. For God, who said, "Let light shine out of darkness," has shone in our hearts to give the light of the knowledge of the glory of God in the face of Jesus Christ.
>
> But we have this treasure in jars of clay, to show that the surpassing power belongs to God and not to us. We are afflicted in every way, but not crushed; perplexed, but not driven to despair; persecuted, but not forsaken; struck down, but not destroyed; always carrying in the body the death of Jesus, so that the life of Jesus may also be manifested in our bodies. For we who live are always being given over to death for Jesus' sake, so that the life of Jesus also may be manifested in our mortal flesh. So death is at work in us, but life in you.
>
> Since we have the same spirit of faith according to what has been written, "I believed, and so I spoke," we also believe, and so we also speak, knowing that he who raised the Lord Jesus will raise us also with Jesus and

bring us with you into his presence. For it is all for your sake, so that as grace extends to more and more people it may increase thanksgiving, to the glory of God.

So we do not lose heart. Though our outer self is wasting away, our inner self is being renewed day by day. For this light momentary affliction is preparing for us an eternal weight of glory beyond all comparison, as we look not to the things that are seen but to the things that are unseen. For the things that are seen are transient, but the things that are unseen are eternal.

In this passage, Paul feels free to include an internal psychological pain, perplexity, in his list of experiences that exemplify "carrying in the body the death of Jesus." Shortly after, he equates this "carrying" with a "light momentary affliction" in which "our outer self is wasting away."

Elsewhere Paul writes (Rom. 8:16-17): "The Spirit himself bears witness with our spirit that we are children of God, and if children, then heirs—heirs of God and fellow heirs with Christ, provided we suffer with him in order that we may also be glorified with him." Dr. N.T. Wright correctly explains verse 17:

This is the fulcrum about which the whole discourse now pivots. Once Paul has established that all those in Christ and indwelt by the Spirit are "children of God," the end of the argument is in sight: If we are God's children, we are also God's heirs. This is the real reason why he implied that Christians were indebted to God (8:12), and it indicates the substance of the paragraph to come. Paul quickly explains in more detail what it means to be God's heirs: It means that one is a fellow heir with the Messiah. As Christians have shared his prayer, as a symptom of their sharing in his sonship, so they will also share in his inheritance. If he is to be Lord of the world, ruling over it with sovereign and saving love, they are to share that rule, bringing redemption to the world that longs for it (cf. 1 Cor 6:2-3; Paul takes this idea for granted, strange though it may be to us, and assumes that his hearers do so too). But, as Jesus himself solemnly warned, there is a cost involved (see Mark 8:34-38). The road to the inheritance, the path to glory (the two are now, at last, seen to be more or less synonymous) lies along the road of suffering.[18]

The rest of the unit of thought that 8:17 falls within extends to 8:30, and passes through discussions of the groaning of creation, the groaning of believers for their resurrection bodies, and the groaning of the Spirit which entails God's providential care for believers through "all things" (8:28). In this passage, the apostle links the necessity of the suffering of believers with their continued existence in the present age. In the mind of the apostle, this age is the age of the curse, where the earth produces

---

[18] N.T. Wright, "Romans", in *The New Interpreter's Bible: Acts – First Corinthians*, vol. 10 (Nashville, TN: Abington, 2002), 594.

thorns and decay. It is the age where human beings can be subject to suffering on account of, e.g.: tribulation, distress, persecution, famine, nakedness, danger, the sword, angels and rulers, things present and things to come, powers, height nor depth, and anything in creation. It is the age where all human beings must live in bodies that will eventually return to dust.

Paul's reflections on these themes are profound, and warrant many books dedicated to them entirely. But the important point for our purposes here is to note: for the apostle, joining in the sufferings of Christ was not simply about being a persecuted minority in society. It was about enduring the effects of the curse; it was about accepting death in all its forms (literal and figurative) from the hand of God, and living in the certain hope that one day we will be redeemed from it, just as Christ has been. Refusing to take up the cross is not essentially about the minority's temptation to take political and social power; refusing the cross is rather essentially repeating the sin of the Garden. Rejecting one's cross is an action rooted in distrust of God's goodness, leading to an attempt to minimize our pain and maximize our happiness by making moral compromises and breaking God's commands.[19]

---

[19] This theme comes very close to Martin Luther's concept of *Anfechtung*, and Dr. David P. Scaer has written a profound summary of Luther's teaching on this subject in "The Concept of Anfechtung in Luther's Thought," *Concordia Theological Quarterly* 47, no. 1 (Jan. 1983): 15-30. Luther's meditations on this idea could help the modern church to much more deeply understand Jesus' command to take up the cross.

RENDER TO CAESAR

Some passages in Jesus' teaching do not directly address violence, but nevertheless become relevant to the issue because they directly address political matters. One such case is the conversion including the famous saying, "render to Caesar what is Caesar's, and to God what is God's," found in all the synoptics, and in Matt. 22:15-22. Dr. Christopher Bryan, in his book *Render to Caesar: Jesus, the Early Church, and the Roman Superpower*, provides the best interpretation of this answer's political significance:

> Aside from Jesus' comment on the motives of those who question him, his initial response takes the form of a request for clarification and information. "Bring me a denarius and let me see it. ... Whose head... is this, and whose title...?" But, of course, the "request" is really a rhetorical trap. "The emperor's," they say. Indeed, they can say nothing else. That, after all, was precisely what many of them disliked about the coin. What then? Disliked or not, the emperor's head and inscription meant that it was the emperor's coin, and according to ancient understanding a ruler's coin was his property. The trap springs. "Give... to the emperor the things that are the emperor's." Jesus' statement is, actually, more forceful than his questioners required, since he has exchanged the rather general word for payment... that they used for a much more precise word...–a word that speaks of payment as "a contractual or other

obligation," or restoration "to an original possessor." The implication is, "Pay up what you owe! Give back to the Emperor what is his!" Pace Horsely, I cannot see how such a response, to such a question, in the situation in which Jesus and his questioners found themselves, can possibly have been heard or intended as "subtle avoidance" or anything of that kind. On the contrary, Jesus' words, once examined, appear in their context to be quite unequivocal. As Morna Hooker correctly points out, Jesus has said that, "however much the inhabitants of Judah dislike it, they cannot escape the authority of Caesar and the obligation it entails."[20]

Dr. Bryan concludes that this teaching fits with the view he defends throughout *Render to Caesar*,[21] viz., that Jesus' view of the political superpowers is the same as that of the biblical Joseph, Daniel, and Ezra. None of these men, it should be noted, were pacifists, nor were they anarchists of any kind.

THE GENTILE RULERS

Another indirectly relevant teaching of Jesus' is his comment about Gentile rulers. In Matthew, this story is found in chapter 20:20-28:

> Then the mother of the sons of Zebedee came up to him with her sons, and kneeling

[20] Bryan, *Render to Caesar* (Oxford: OUP, 2005), 45.

[21] Bryan, 46.

before him she asked him for something. And he said to her, "What do you want?" She said to him, "Say that these two sons of mine are to sit, one at your right hand and one at your left, in your kingdom." Jesus answered, "You do not know what you are asking. Are you able to drink the cup that I am to drink?" They said to him, "We are able." He said to them, "You will drink my cup, but to sit at my right hand and at my left is not mine to grant, but it is for those for whom it has been prepared by my Father." And when the ten heard it, they were indignant at the two brothers. But Jesus called them to him and said, "You know that the rulers of the Gentiles lord it over them, and their great ones exercise authority over them. It shall not be so among you. But whoever would be great among you must be your servant, and whoever would be first among you must be your slave, even as the Son of Man came not to be served but to serve, and to give his life as a ransom for many."

The parallel texts are phrased slightly differently. In Mark 10:42 the text runs thus:

And Jesus called them to him and said to them, "You know that those who are considered rulers of the Gentiles lord it over them, and their great ones exercise authority over them...."

And in Luke 22:24-25:

> A dispute also arose among them, as to which of them was to be regarded as the greatest. And he said to them, "The kings of the Gentiles exercise lordship over them, and those in authority over them are called benefactors. ..."

The most important phrases to discuss are "lord it over" (κατακυριεύω), "exercise authority" (κατεξουσιάζω), "exercise lordship" (κυριεύω) and "in authority" (ἐξουσιάζω).

With regard to the first word κατακυριεύω, 1 Pet. 5:3 also commands elders not to do this. Yet, the NT regards elders as having actual authority over their churches (e.g., 1 Cor. 16:16; 1 Pet. 5:2; Heb. 13:7, 17; 1 Tim. 2:12-3:7, noting especially 3:5, which draws a direct parallel between the authority of a parent and that of an elder). Jesus and Peter both must mean, then, a tyrannical kind of abusive authority, not authority as such, which is reflected in translations such as "lord it over" and "domineer."

The second word, κατεξουσιάζω, is used in the apocryphal *Acts of Thomas* 98 of a man attempting to rape a woman, and in Tatian's Letter to the Greeks (15) of matter's attempt to dominate the spirit (which for Tatian is clearly an evil thing). Thus the word can certainly have connotations of a kind of tyrannizing, an exercising of power over someone or something without a right to do so, rather than entailing an ethically neutral holding of authority.

The third word, κυριεύω, can also sometimes seem to have the connotation of pejorative form of ruling, something more like domineering.[22] Given that Paul disclaims doing this to the faith of the Corinthians in 2 Cor. 1:24, while nevertheless claiming to have real authority over them in 1 Cor. 4:18-21; 2 Cor. 10:8; and 13:1-3, there is some evidence the word can have a pejorative connotation in the NT corpus.

The fourth word, ἐξουσιάζω, can be used in a positive setting, as it is in 1 Cor. 7:4, where Paul affirms spouses have this over their spouses' bodies. On the other hand, Paul can use it with an apparently negative connotation, as in 1 Cor. 6:12: "I will not be enslaved by anything." The first use by Paul entails having ἐξουσιάζω is not intrinsically wrong, and the second shows the word can be used with a pejorative connotation.

All of the words Jesus uses to describe activities common to Gentile rulers, in other words, can have a pejorative meaning. Alongside this lexical point, we must also recognize Jesus affirmed authority in various ways. He taught it would be present even in the age to come (Matt. 19:28): "Jesus said to them, 'Truly, I say to you, in the new world, when the Son of Man will sit on his glorious throne, you who have followed me will also sit on twelve thrones, judging the twelve tribes of Israel.'" He also taught that disciples had the authority to excommunicate recalcitrant church members (Matt. 18:17): "If he refuses to listen to them, tell it to the church. And if he refuses to listen even to the church, let him be to you as a Gentile and a tax collector." He said there would be scribes in the kingdom (Matt. 13:52), who by definition have the authority of experts in their religious community. In fact, nowhere in

---

[22] BDAG suggests Philo, *Legum Allegoriarum* 3, 187 and *Testament of Simeon* 3:2 as examples of this usage.

the OT and the NT is authority per se criticized as immoral. The natural conclusion to draw for this pericope is that Jesus is saying his disciples should not "rule" anyone in the pejorative senses these words have. But that leaves open the possibility of righteous rule by disciples.

It is worth noting, as a final comment on this passage, that the sentiment Jesus expresses is not original to him. Arguably, it appears in Ps. 58:1-2:

> Do you indeed decree what is right, you gods?
> Do you judge the children of man uprightly?
> No, in your hearts you devise wrongs;
> your hands deal out violence on earth.

As well as Ps. 82:1-4:

> God has taken his place in the divine council;
> in the midst of the gods he holds judgment:
> "How long will you judge unjustly
> and show partiality to the wicked? Selah
> Give justice to the weak and the fatherless;
> maintain the right of the afflicted and the destitute.
> Rescue the weak and the needy;
> deliver them from the hand of the wicked."

And the observation of the Preacher in Eccl. 4:1:

> Again I saw all the oppressions that are done under the sun. And behold, the tears of the oppressed, and they had no one to comfort them! On the side of their oppressors there was power, and there was no one to comfort them.

In other words, Jesus says nothing more than what the OT has already taught, which is that it is commonplace for authorities to abuse their power. This does not mean it believed this was an absolute and fixed law of behaviour for even Gentile magistrates; in fact, the OT contains several stories where the acts of Gentile kings receive approval (Pharaoh in Joseph's day; Nebuchadnezzar after his conversion; Cyrus' decree that the Jews could return home; etc.).[23] It is not a rule in general, but the abusive kind of rule that Jesus forbids his to followers, as well as the more fundamental attitude of pride that such abuse flows from.

TAKING THE SWORD

As we noted in the first chapter, when Jesus said to Peter (Matt. 26:52), "Put your sword back into its place. For all who take the sword will perish by the sword", he uttered a common piece of timeless wisdom. This statement finds OT precedents, where it could not be pacifistic. What it really means is something people have truly recognized forever: that unjust aggression provokes vengeance from others. At least in the OT, however, this was not taken to mean that state coercion could never be effective. Further, it would find clear application in the case of revolutionaries and the seditious. These people, the OT taught, were very likely to meet a nasty end as a result of state vengeance. It is this aspect of the saying in particular which directly applies in Jesus' context, for Peter's violent

---

[23] On this theme, note C. John Collins, "Echoes of Aristotle in Romans 2:14–15: Or, Maybe Abimelech Was Not So Bad After All", *Journal of Markets & Morality* 13, no. 1 (2010): 141-142.

act was committed against deputies of the state, and no doubt had a zealot holy war ideology as its engine. But Jesus knew the zealot agenda had no chance of succeeding against the might of the first century Roman empire. All those who took up the sword in that sense and context would surely die by it. And sadly, because they did not heed his warning, that is exactly what happened to Jewish zealot movements in 70 AD.

THE CROSS AS ARGUMENT FOR PACIFISM

By far, the most common event in Jesus' life used to justify pacifism is his submission to crucifixion. The basic claim is that his refusal to defend himself was an expression of his condemnation of violence in general. He regarded dying as preferable to killing in all situations, and so also in that situation.

But there are problems with this argument. Interpreting the intentions behind actions can often be difficult, for the same actions can be motivated by very different intentions. And such is the case with being willing to die. Granting that Jesus willingly suffered death, a number of possible explanations could provide the rationale for this act, without entailing pacifism.

One such motive would be to provide the propitiation for the sins of mankind. While some scholars have attempted to refute this possibility by denying the NT teaches Christ's death was a propitiation, that attempt should be regarded as a failure. Dr. John R. W. Stott's masterpiece, *The Cross of Christ*, notes some evidence that Jesus himself taught this was a purpose for his death. Referring to the Last Supper where Jesus explains the purpose of his death as being for the forgiveness of sins

(Matt. 26:26-28), Dr. Stott writes: "Here is Jesus' view of his death. It is the divinely appointed sacrifice by which the new covenant with its promise of forgiveness will be ratified."[24] And noting Jesus' prayer in Gethsemane that "this cup" pass from him (cf. Matt. 26:39), he explains that the "cup" had an OT background that indicated it symbolized God's wrath (cf. Job 21:20; Isa. 51:17-22; Ps. 75:8), which Jesus would have known.[25] When we lift our gaze from Jesus' own words to the NT as a whole, the earliest interpretation of Jesus' teaching, we see that the cross was propitiatory is certain.[26] So this provides one motivation for Jesus' death.

The logic of just war theory provides another. Given Jesus' historical situation, where he knew very well that God did not wish to save him by means of legions of angels, and where his human followers had no political power, Jesus could not actually wage a successful war against the Herods, the Sanhedrin, and the Roman

---

[24] John R. W. Stott, *The Cross of Christ: 20th Anniversary Edition* (Downer's Grove: InterVarsity Press, 2006), 72.

[25] Stott, 78-79.

[26] For example, Rom 3:24-26, where God in forbearance overlooked sins committed before Jesus' death because he was going to look at and deal squarely with them in that event. The implication is that the sins provoked God's wrath but that he held it until he unleashed it at the crucifixion. Recent works have provided extensive biblical and philosophical defenses of this position, and readers are encouraged to consult them if they want to pursue this issue further: Jeremy Treat, *The Crucified King: Atonement and Kingdom in Biblical and Systematic Theology* (Grand Rapids: Zondervan, 2014); and Adonis Vidu, *Atonement, Law, and Justice: The Cross in Historical and Cultural Contexts* (Grand Rapids: Baker Academic, 2014). Many contemporary criticisms of penal substitution are directly motivated by doctrines related to pacifism, wherein writers contend that attributing violence or retribution to God contradicts the non-violent nature of Jesus' gospel.

empire. He had no prospect of success. Further, in the system of human positive law that he lived under, Jesus had no political authority. These two facts alone mean, by just war logic, that he could not rightly fight the state when its agents came to arrest him. Just war criteria demanded his surrender at this point.

Pacifists will also sometimes suggest that Jesus' death at the hands of the Romans somehow entails that government *per se* is always unjust, or at least that capital punishment is such. But of course, this does not follow with any kind of necessity from Jesus' death. This conclusion must be read into his death first before it can be read out of it. For even in Jesus' day people were well aware that unjust killing could happen (e.g., there were OT laws against murder for a reason) without concluding that capital punishment was therefore always unjust.

PROBLEMS WITH PACIFIST MORAL RATIONALES

We return once again to the six major moral rationales given for pacifism:

1. Cycle of violence
2. Limits of human knowledge
3. Immorality of punishment and vengefulness
4. Unloving character of violence
5. Utopian character of violence
6. Hierarchy as intrinsically dominative

The texts discussed above, upon close analysis, provide no positive support for any of these arguments. Some of the passages, in fact, contradict them: Jesus teaches his disciples to practice excommunication, suggesting he disagrees with 2, 3, and 6. Other texts provide difficulty for the remaining reasons. For example, Jesus predicted that Rome would soon come to crush the Jewish revolt (e.g., Luke 23:27-31). This contradicts 1, for it entails the imperial response would be definitive. It also would seem to undermine 5, for it presents a case where God sends non-eschatological (i.e., human mediated) justice to nevertheless definitively accomplish a political judgment. Perhaps, too, this event shows the consistency of love with violent judgment. For while Jesus appeals to God as the perfect exemplar of the virtue of enemy-love in the Sermon on the Mount (Matt. 5:45, 48), he is also quite clear that God is the ultimate agent behind the coming Roman desolation of Jerusalem (Matt. 21:38-44; cf. Luke 20:13-16).

Regardless of the positive case against moral pacifism from Jesus' teaching, though, there is a distinct lack of evidence in favour of it. And as with the NT data outside of Jesus' teaching, none of the texts used to support non-violence seem to be ceremonial or symbolic in nature.

And this brings us back to our beginning, when we noted the significance of "Semantic Axiom Number One", and Ockham's razor. That is, if we can find one sufficient explanation for a phenomenon, we should not look for more. And after this survey, we can see that affirmation of the principles found in the OT and natural law can explain all of Jesus' teachings relevant to the use of violence. We need not take recourse to a new pacifistic motive for his words.

IV:

THE POST-APOSTOLIC CHURCH

SO FAR we have only discussed transhistorical principles and biblical exegesis. But another important part of this debate requires discussion. In the final analysis, the strongest argument for pacifism comes not from the subjects we have already discussed, but from the early post-apostolic church. It is there where we find the first truly pacifistic Christians. And the eventual widespread presence of this opinion among believers does press a question upon historians: how did this happen? Pacifists have a straightforward answer: the widespread pacifism of the early church is explained through faithful transmission of apostolic tradition, which in turn derived from the founder of the religion, Jesus Christ himself.

But we have already argued that this is an erroneous reading of the scriptures, and certainly has no foundation in timeless natural law. This leaves an important historical question for non-pacifists open: how do we explain the widespread pacifism of the early church?

The non-pacifist is admittedly at a disadvantage here: there is very little literature from the earliest days of the apostolic church that has relevance to this subject. Justin Martyr is arguably the first Christian to have enunciated a kind of pacifism, and he is followed by Irenaeus, Tertullian, and Origen, probably among others.[1] Between the writing of the last New Testament book and Justin's writings there is probably around at least half a century where no strong evidence exists for either pacifism or a denial of it. Thus, from the very beginning, the non-pacifist is restrained to give only speculations about what might have happened. There is no early church text that says "The entire church became pacifist in 140 AD"; if something like that did happen, we will only be able to detect it indirectly.

Yet, if one agrees with the reading of the New Testament already provided, there are certain historical facts that might indicate how the shift happened. We will provide some of them below, though there are probably even more factors that may have enabled the transition in reality. A rough heuristic for sorting the various types of factors is as follows: causes arising from perennial aspects of life, from the church's relation to Gentiles, from its relation to Jews, and causes internal to Christianity.

---

[1] This section will take for granted the pacifist reading of the early church, both because it actually seems to be mostly correct, and because providing a harmonization of the non-pacifist reading of the NT with the pacifist reading of the early church would make the case for the just war tradition even stronger. However, while accepting that "majority pacifist" view of the early church, any honest survey cannot overlook that there were Christians in the military from very early on. Tertullian almost brags at one point in his writings that Christians fight alongside pagans in the imperial forces: see *Apology* 42. However this is to be explained–pacifists say it is a failure to live up to Christian teaching–it must be explained.

PERENNIAL FACTORS

1. *Passage of time:* As noted above, a significant period of time passes before the first text that supports pacifism. With any tradition passed through history, the passage of time allows for greater chances of error spreading in the transmission. Even within the NT, while the apostles were still living, there are examples of ideas spreading that were mistakenly attributed to Jesus or the apostles (John 21:20-23; 2 Thess. 2:1-2; Galatians in its entirety). How much more likely would the spread of error become once the apostles had passed from the scene?

2. *Unnatural violence:* Human beings naturally recoil from violence, especially violence against other people. This natural tendency is designed by God to limit violence; yet God also expects us to use our reason, and recognize when the greater good requires morally discriminating violence. However, the right use of reason can be difficult at times, as our passions can overwhelm our rational capacities if we do not train ourselves rightly, or receive bad training from others. The general (good) disposition to avoid violence, along with poor training in wisdom and virtue, could therefore incline any person in any age towards a pacifistic stance. Certainly it could do so to a first or second century Christian, especially given a superficial reading of Jesus' teachings.

3. *Complex subject:* The ethics of violence is intrinsically complicated. It requires some grasp of human nature, of the nature of justice, retribution, politics, God, wisdom, and the proper hierarchy of values. Further, when one has to factor in special revelation of some kind, the issue becomes even more difficult: then the ethical subject must have some knowledge of texts, interpretive rules, possibly

85

knowledge of the original languages, and mastery with concepts like progressive revelation. With any subject, the more complicating factors that are involved, the more likely error in judgment becomes.

4. *Minority tendencies:* In any time or place, minority groups on the receiving end of persecution can tend to slide into a ghetto mentality. The pacifist or Anabaptist approach to in-group/out-group relations is a perennial option, and the early church was in a situation highly conducive to its adoption, suffering great persecution at times.

5. *Hazards of war:* War, being on the edge of legality and political order, has always provided occasion for sin. It is therefore unsurprising that people especially concerned with moral purity might regard war with ever increasing suspicion, to the point where they become convinced that it is intrinsically disordered.

CAUSES RELATED TO GENTILES

1. *Abuse of execution:* From very early on, Roman governors executed Christians for stubbornness and various other charges. The Christians regarded these penalties as unjust. It would not be surprising if the church, being faced with such systemic injustice, made a blanket judgment about all state violence, forbidding Christians to participate in a practice that was so often in their own experience clearly evil. Further, the fact that Christians were still being executed during the periods when Christian soldiers might be ordered to perform executions would bring another factor into the mix, that of the proper behaviour of Christians toward their fellow

believers. This would only tend to push the church further against all capital punishment.

2. *The charge of insurrection:* The Christians were constantly under suspicion of, and often openly charged with, being insurrectionists. Given the heinous punishments that would follow from such a conviction, the Christians had every reason to emphasize how non-violent they were. And of course, the polar opposite of revolutionary violence would be absolute pacifism. One can easily imagine the great motivation the early church would have had to argue the Christian religion was intrinsically pacifist.

3. *Compulsory idolatry:* Non-pacifist scholars of the early church have sometimes tried to argue that the compulsory idolatry involved in Roman military practices was the main objection the church had to soldiering. This is probably incorrect, but nevertheless, this aspect of military service could certainly incline many Christians towards blanket condemnation. Once it became clear policy that Christianity was not a form of Judaism, and so not deserving of the status of exemptions that Jews had from participation in Roman religion, Christians would have increasing trouble being part of Roman society. While there were probably *de facto* exceptions made for Christian soldiers on the ground, still the official attitude would not have been one of making exceptions. This general hostility probably would encourage fewer Christians to be soldiers, which would in turn reinforce the perception that Christianity was a pacifistic religion.

CAUSES RELATED TO JUDAISM

1. *Loss of contact with Jewish roots:* Dr. David Instone-Brewer writes about the connection of the church to Judaism:

The Early Church lost touch with its Jewish roots in or before 70 C.E. Various passages in the NT suggest that Christians were excommunicated from the synagogue before the NT canon was completed, and certainly before 70 C.E. This marked the beginning of the loss of Jewish culture within the Church. A few Christian groups such as the Nazarenes and Ebionites continued to follow Jewish customs, but these soon died out. The Church very quickly forgot its Jewish roots, and thereby lost contact with much of the Jewish background of the NT writings.[2]

This loss of Jewish context would cause problems for understanding Jesus' teaching, for he was directly engaging with ideas from the context. Indeed, with regard to the Sermon on the Mount in particular, it has been difficult for many interpreters to grasp that Jesus is responding to problematic practices in Palestinian Jewish culture, and not the Law itself, no doubt partly because that culture is less known than the Old Testament, especially to non-historians. But in addition, loss of contact with Jewish interpreters could increase the chances of misunderstanding the OT. Though in many ways their understanding was incorrect, nevertheless the disciplined way in which Rabbinic Judaism carefully approached the OT could certainly have helped Christians understand their own book. The loss of conversation partners within that

---

[2] David Instone-Brewer, *Divorce and Remarriage in the Bible: the Social and Literary Context* (Grand Rapids: Eerdmans, 2002), 238.

tradition could easily lead to an impoverishment of knowledge on the part of the church.

2. *Hostility toward Judaism:* At the same time, the Church was on hostile terms with Judaism from the very start. They were forced to dispute with those who stood in the line of the Pharisees, who rejected Jesus' claims to be the OT's promised Messiah. The church was therefore highly motivated to prove their religion was truer and better than Judaism, for they wanted to convert both the Jews as well as undecided onlookers who might be tempted to become Jews rather than Christians. Yet, as I noted in a previous chapter, Dr. Allison argued that this motive inclined Christians to try to read the Sermon on the Mount against Judaism in general, and even the correct understanding of OT in particular, insofar as Judaism held on to a proper interpretation of it. In other words, if the Jews argued for non-pacifism from the OT, the Christians might be tempted to argue that the New Testament religion was better and purer precisely in being pacifistic. The Jewish-Christian hostility would feed the divisions on this matter, and tend to exaggerate differences.

3. *Misreading of prophecies:* One possible instance of this point is in an early approach to the prophecies of Isaiah chapter 2, where the prophet foresees the future age when the Law would go out from Zion and judge between nations, leading to their beating their swords into ploughshares, i.e., world peace. Beginning with Justin, Christians appealed to their own pacifistic behaviour as the fulfillment of this prophecy, to prove that Christianity was the fulfillment of the Old Testament, even over against Judaism. Reading Isaiah in its original context does not naturally lead to this interpretation, though familiarity with

Justin's kind of application may lead contemporary Christian readers astray in this regard. Isaiah predicts an age of total global peace, not an age of a minority religious movement refusing to serve in the militaries of nations who are still at war with each other. Nevertheless, Christians did argue along Justin's lines, and probably partly for the reasons suggested in the point immediately above.

4. *Quasi-Marcionism:* This separation from, and hostility to, Jewish religion, coupled with the hermeneutical techniques of the pagan Alexandrinian school, in some cases led to near-Marcionite approaches to the OT. Dr. Ronald J. Sider brings attention to one such passage (though he does not describe it this way) in his *The Early Church on Killing: A Comprehensive Sourcebook on War, Abortion, And Capital Punishment*, from Origen's *Contra Celsus* 7.19:4

> It is sufficient at present to refer to the manner in which in the Psalms the just man is represented as saying, among other things, Every morning will I destroy the wicked of the land; that I may cut off all workers of iniquity from the city of Jehovah. Judge, then, from the words and spirit of the speaker, whether it is conceivable that, after having in the preceding part of the Psalm, as any one may read for himself, uttered the noblest thoughts and purposes, he should in the sequel, according to the literal rendering of his words, say that in the morning, and at no other period of the day, he would destroy all sinners from the earth, and leave none of them

alive, and that he would slay every one in Jerusalem who did iniquity. And there are many similar expressions to be found in the law, as this, for example: We left not anything alive.[3]

The idea that the thought of judging sinners would be ignoble suggests a subtle moral criticism of political judgment, which would entail a rejection of moral principles the OT supports. From this to Marcionism there is but a hair's breadth. And indeed, insofar as such attitudes were prevalent, even if only unconsciously, amongst Christians, the wide proselytizing successes of Marcionism are unsurprising. Marcion, of course, was a pacifist, and rejected the entire OT as the revelation of another god.

CAUSES WITHIN CHRISTIANITY

1. *Easy mistake:* Non-pacifists do need to admit that the tenor and surface meaning of Jesus' teaching, especially in the texts discussed above, can easily lend themselves to a pacifistic interpretation. It is not at all surprising that the early church made this mistake, and that interpreters continue to do so today. Jesus really did teach about, and emphasize dramatically, practices such as mercy and love. He had almost nothing to say about the duties of magistrates. If the average Christian were to memorize Jesus' most memorable and significant (for daily life) teachings, they probably would memorize the Sermon on the Mount. And if that was all they memorized, and did

---

[3] Sider, *The Early Church on Killing* (Grand Rapids: Baker Academic, 2012), 75.

not think deeply about the context of the teaching along the lines we have argued above, pacifism would probably seem like the obvious import of Jesus' words.

2. *Limited knowledge of the Bible:* We also have to remember that the early church lived before the age of Gutenberg. Most churches did not have complete copies of the canon, and certainly most individuals did not. It is highly likely that a large number of Christians heard only select portions of scripture, rather than the entire scope of it. The loss of the full counsel of the word of God could mean a loss of vital context, and therefore misinterpretation.

3. *Wooden and rigid hermeneutic:* Early Christians sometimes fell into rather rigid and strict interpretations of biblical teachings. *The Shepherd of Hermas*, a pseudepigraphon believed by many in the early church to be inspired scripture, taught that post-baptismal sin could be forgiven only once. Tertullian taught that remarriage was improper even after the death of one's spouse. More to the point, Dr. Sider notes Lactantius criticizing just war ethics in *The Divine Institutes* 6.9 and 6.18, an approach that would entail moral criticism of the OT, and again return us to a sort of Marcionism.[4] One can sympathize with Christians of any age who, looking upon the moral compromises both unbelievers and professing believers inevitably make, read the demands of scripture in the most unyielding of ways. But we also must recognize that this attitude is a distortion of Scripture just as much as its opposite, the loosening of demands beyond their natural meaning. Pacifism easily qualifies as a rigid overinterpretation of some of Jesus' commands, and fits into this general harsh trend.

---

[4] Sider, 109.

4. *General non-violent practice*: As a matter of statistics, most Christians were not magistrates or soldiers. As a consequence, most Christians would have no occasion in which to be physically violent. Further, Christians who happened to follow just war principles would also refuse to revolt against the state, or to fight in wars that were clearly unjust. The result of all this is that one could legitimately generalize, and say that Christians as a rule are not violent. Such a generalization might easily slip into a different conclusion, that Christians were as a rule not violent because their teaching absolutely prohibited it.

5. *Cross-pollination:* The early church communicated a great deal with itself. This includes the big thinkers of the church, who would naturally be more respected and trusted in their teachings. Irenaeus read Justin, as did Tertullian and Origen. And Justin probably was a pacifist. Is it surprising, then, that those who followed in his footsteps would have taken his view? No. Further, outside the issue of pacifism, there are several doctrines and practices that spread throughout the church and were taken to be apostolic, though they probably did not originate with the apostles. One example would be Chiliasm (or, depending on your opinion, non-Chiliasm).[5] Another would be the virtually semi-Pelagian approach to free will that a lot of the apologists took.[6] The shift to monoepiscopacy happened without any explicit notice,

---

[5] See Dr. Charles Hill's account in *Regnum Caelorum: Patterns of Millennial Thought in Early Christianity* (Oxford: OUP, 1992).

[6] See Dr. Alister McGrath's discussion of this point in his book, *Iustitia Dei: A History of the Christian Doctrine of Justification,* 3rd ed. (Cambridge: CUP, 2005), 33-38.

though a shift it was.[7] The disagreement over the date of Easter implies either that the apostles taught different dates, in which case the belief that one date was mandated for all churches was very likely an error, or that they taught one date, in which case one of the camps was in error in believing the apostles taught the other date, or else that they mandated no dates, entailing that both camps were wrong. And one early change from NT practice is visible in the catechumenate: an institution that did not exist during the time of the apostles, but became widespread very soon after. All of these movements suggest that the spread of influence could be very fast, and even for ideas that were not apostolic though they soon were taken to be. Pacifism could be just another example of this.

6. *Beliefs about Christian soldiers:* Of course, one might object: would not these early pacifistic Christians have known about Christian soldiers in good standing with the church, if there were any such individuals? Probably; but they may have imagined most such soldiers were not violent, and so technically in obedience to the commands of Jesus as they interpreted them. They may have acknowledged a few were violent, but regarded them as sinful and in the minority. These would have been erroneous assumptions, but not impossible ones to imagine them making. And indeed, we must note that Tertullian, who in many places could speak of Christians as pacifist without qualification, in his *Apology* (42), can say of his fellow Christians to his pagan neighbours: "We sail with you, and fight with you, and till the ground with

---

[7] See Dr. James Tunstead Burtchaell's meticulous analysis of this issue in *From Synagogue to Church: Public Services and Offices in the Earliest Christian Communities* (Cambridge: CUP, 1992).

you."[8] That he does not constantly qualify his unqualified pacifistic statements does not make this statement any less significant, though it does raise interesting questions about why he did not modify his language appropriately, and about whether historians should qualify similar statements among other early Christian pacifists.

7. *Idealistic fathers:* The final point to make regarding the early church is that most of the pacifistic texts we have come from church rules and Christian teachers. Both kinds of texts are written by people who are concerned to defend and shore up the distinctively Christian identity of their churches. Yet, as in other ages and places, such motivations can sometimes lead to a desire for the church to be a perfected society, and an imagination that it already is one. This can lead to both denials of on-the-ground divergence from the preferred ideal, and a ratcheting up of the preached standards for laypeople. The laypeople, as in other ages, may have taken a different view on the matters, not because they were simply unfaithful, but because they disagreed with the interpretations their intellectual heavyweights offered. This could have been true in the case of pacifism as well. It would certainly explain the persistent presence of Christians in the army. It would not be the first time that laypeople disregarded the opinions of intellectuals in the face of practical realities.

---

[8] This reference comes from Sider, *The Early Church on Killing*, 56.

V:

CONCLUDING REFLECTIONS

IN THIS book I have attempted to answer the question "Was Jesus a pacifist?" in the negative. The argument began with a survey of four aspects of Jesus' background: natural law, the context of literary conventions, social context, and the Old Testament. These four aspects pointed to the conclusion that Jesus' teaching was not pacifistic. The first chapter ended by presenting the various kinds of pacifisms, and the reasons offered to support these kinds, to facilitate comparison. That is, once the reasons for non-violence were clear, we could check to see whether the source documents for the Christian religion held those reasons. The second chapter began by noting that the background for Jesus' teaching did not cohere with pacifism. It continued by surveying the NT documents, written after Jesus' teaching had first been given. This aimed at discovering if Jesus' teaching, intervening as it does between OT and NT, produced effects that would suggest he had departed from what his background would lead us to expect. The second chapter found that all four aspects of his background continued into the age of the New Testament. This made the conclusion that Jesus was not a pacifist even more likely.

The third chapter of the book attempted to explain the teachings and actions of Jesus that pacifists claim support their position, and found that none of these teachings or actions do so. Finally, the fourth chapter provided some possible explanations as to why the early church misunderstood what those teachings were really about, and turned to embrace pacifism. Of course, many may remain unconvinced, and the brevity of the analysis may provide some room for that posture. Yet, hopefully, the argument has at least provided a reason for a moment of pause.

Before bringing this discussion to a close, a few further thoughts deserve reflection.

NEVERTHELESS

Perhaps remarkably, Dr. John Howard Yoder includes the just war tradition in his book *Nevertheless*, as what he calls "The Pacifism of the Honest Study Cases."[1] This is not entirely misleading. By subordinating war and violence to justice, the just war tradition does substantially reduce the possible uses of violence open to state and non-state actors from those permitted by a totally Machievellian *realpolitik*. Indeed, one can reasonably see how, if everyone followed just war principles, which are simply implications of the virtue of justice, there would never be another war. In fact, this is arguably the natural implication of the eschatological vision of Isa. 2, the very one that early church pacifists appealed to: since it is submission to the Law that brings about peace, and that Law taught not pacifism but just war principles, the coming age of peace

---

[1] John Howard Yoder, *Nevertheless: The Varieties and Shortcomings of Religious Pacifism* (Scottdale, PA: Herald Press, 1992), 22-28.

shall come about not because people refuse to join the army, but because all nations will be just, and therefore give no cause for war in the first place.

JUST WAR AND THE TWO KINGDOMS

Most significant theological conversions do not come about because of mere arguments. They almost always are accompanied by changes of imagination and desire. They come about because people catch a different vision of the whole world, and begin to see the parts in light of that whole. So while the foregoing argument has attempted to provide better parts than the pacifist narrative, it may seem rather piecemeal apart from the natural whole. Thus a brief sweep of that whole deserves some mention. That whole is the two kingdoms vision of magisterial Protestantism.

The two kingdoms vision begins with a distinction between the internal and the external, the soul and the body. This is a distinction that all cultures have acknowledged, and so does not need much defense, and will receive none here. Two kingdoms theology argues that God rules these two realms differently. The internal he rules directly, immediately, in the hearts of believers by the power of the Word through the Spirit. The external he rules indirectly and mediately, through various human agents, in a way that can be resisted.

Intertwined with this distinction are other familiar distinctions. One of these is the Law/Gospel distinction. According to the two kingdoms approach, the believer is justified by faith, and so internally is put beyond the judgment of the law. Being justified, the law no longer has the power to condemn. But externally, in behaviour, the believer still sins, and so can still be subject to the law.

Further, unbelievers are certainly still subject to the law. The Law continues to have force because people continue to sin, and the preservation of the common good of society requires some coercive restraint upon behaviour. Yet, the power of the Gospel is not unrelated to external life. Rather, it transforms it organically, from the heart outward. Indeed, the entire purpose of the Gospel is to effect this transformation: grace is aimed not at the destruction or replacement of nature, but its restoration and perfection according to its original telos.

The external kingdom, ruled mediately by humans and according to Law, has an intrinsic nature, one that has traditionally been summarized into the "Three Estates": family, church, and state. Genesis provides us with origin of these estates. God created humanity and directed them to be fruitful and multiply, originating the family and marriage and its function of procreation. He further told them to take dominion over the earth, bringing about the second function of the family, that of production and business, i.e., economics. As the likenesses of God, these human beings also had the task and joy of worshipping God, and doing so as the social beings that they are.[2] This

---

[2] In an instructive article on the ANE context of the concepts of "likeness" and "image," Peter J. Gentry explains regarding the distinct meaning of the terms:

> Particularly instructive for Gen 1:26-28 is the usage of the words "likeness" and "image" in the Tell Fakhariyeh Inscription. Inscribed on a large statue of King Hadduyith`î of Gozan, a city in what is now eastern Syria, is an Akkadian-Aramaic bilingual text from the tenth or ninth century B.C. The text is divided thematically in two sections. The first half focuses on the role of the king as a supplicant and worshipper of his god and is headed in the Aramaic text by דמותא,

is a description of the church in its original state. Finally, the human family, eventually to be composed of many smaller families, would naturally have to organize these tasks, and organize the relations of the various families together. This is the task of politics, ordering the polis toward the common good.

The three estates are just a part of nature, and it is nature that the Gospel, the internal kingdom, will one day restore by grace. Until that day, however, sin remains, and so heteronomous law is needed. And in the temporal,

---

equivalent of the Hebrew דמות. The second half focuses on the majesty and power of the king in his role in relation to his subjects. This is headed in the Aramaic text by the word צלמא, equivalent of the Hebrew צלם. While both terms can and do refer to the statue of the king, each has a different nuance. …

Given the normal meanings of "image" and "likeness" in the cultural and linguistic setting of Old Testament and the ancient Near East, "likeness" specifies a relationship between God and humans such that *'ādām* can be described as the son of God, and "image" describes a relationship between God and humans such that *'ādām* can be described as a servant king. Although both terms specify the divine-human relationship, the first focuses on the human in relation to God and the second focuses on the human in relation to the world. These would be understood to be relationships characterized by faithfulness and loyal love, obedience and trust—exactly the character of relationships specified by covenants after the fall. In this sense the divine image entails a covenant relationship between God and humans on the one hand, and between humans and the world on the other. In describing a divine-human relationship, the terms in Gen 1:26-28 correspond precisely to the usage of the same words in the Tell Fakhariyah Inscription. (Peter J. Gentry, "Kingdom Through Covenant: Humanity as the Divine Image", *Southern Baptist Journal of Theology* 12, no. 1 [Spring 2008]: 28-29).

external kingdom, order is maintained by that law. In the present age, when some forces and individuals aimed at disorder are willing to act in extreme ways, sometimes coercion is required to maintain the common good against threats. Decisions of when to use this common good rightly reside with the whole to which that common good belongs, i.e., the polis. Hence, as long as there is sin, natural justice dictates that the polis has the right to use force, and to delegate that use to magistrates and their officers. Grace, though in many cases eliminating the need for such force, does not entirely do so; nor does it require force to be abandoned in the face of severe threats to the political order. Rather, it normally works by reshaping the hearts, and so the behaviour, of citizens and strangers, so that the common good can be reached with less and less heteronomous imposition, and more and more natural obedience to the order of charity.

This is a quick summary of the two kingdoms approach to politics and violence, but it should be sufficient to sketch the big picture. Within this context, just war tradition makes sense as a theological implication of the more basic principles, that the present time is characterized by the overlapping of the two ages, and that the age to come resides primarily in the internal, in the inner man; the external can come to signify the internal change to a greater degree, but until the day when all things are renewed, it must be regulated by the systems and order of the old age, the age with sin and so with need of coercion to maintain a minimum of justice.

MAGISTERIAL PROTESTANTISM

One implication of this larger argument is that the magisterial Protestants saw something that the early church, the peace-Anabaptists, and even some contemporary critical scholars, have been unable to see, i.e., that Jesus was neither a pacifist nor an anarchist. Why is it that these early modern figures were able to see this, when so many were unable?

The answer is ultimately in their method. The magisterial Reformers were humanists; they were taught to seek for the truth in the sources, interpreted naturally and honestly according to authorial intention in historical context. They were also scripturalists; they believed they had to submit to the entire counsel of the Word of God, not just arbitrarily chosen canons within the canon. They understood the significance of the temporal good (they do not have the title "magisterial" for nothing), though they did not make it the ultimate good (and so did not collapse the two kingdoms, or the two ages, into one, as the Roman Catholic and Anabaptist options have done).

The result was that they saw the points that have been made in this book. They saw that the OT really did contradict pacifism; they saw the continuity of the NT with the OT, and of both with natural law. If nothing else, we hope that the present study will cause some today to see the wisdom in the approach of the Reformers, and to deeply consider whether they might still have something to say to us.

APPENDIX:
A BRIEF REJOINDER TO HAUERWAS ON LEWIS AND PACIFISM

C. S. Lewis has been the subject of much ink, and with good reason: he ranks with the best apologists of the 20th century, if not as the best. But he did not write only as an apologist, at least not if we conceive that term narrowly. He did not contend only for distinctively Christian doctrines; he also entered the fray on a number of contentious social issues. One such topic was war. In a post for the Calvinist International, I drew from Lewis' essay on the subject of pacifism, and I would like to revisit it.[1]

A brief internet search for the Don's essay will bring up a number of critiques, which should not surprise us given the way Lewis has shaped the last 60 years or so of evangelicalism. However one particular critique comes from a theologian who is himself something of a celebrity, Dr. Stanley Hauerwas.[2] Dr. Hauerwas' essay

---

[1] "Lewis on the Pitfalls and Pathways of Moral Reasoning," The Calvinist International July 14, 2014, https://calvinistinternational.com/2014/07/14/lewis-on-the-pitfalls-and-pathways-of-moral-reasoning/ (accessed on November 7, 2016).

[2] It can be found as "Man of War: Why C.S. Lewis Was Not a Pacifist," ABC Religion and Ethics, August 24, 2012,

represents a growing contingent among evangelicals and post-evangelicals known sometimes as "missional" Christians, sometimes as neo-Anabaptists. John Howard Yoder lies below (and sometimes on) the surface of this group's thinking about violence. Prof. Lewis, in contrast, stands downstream from what TCI has often called classical Protestantism. My purpose in this post is to mount a brief defense of Prof. Lewis' position. If successful, my hope is that evangelicals might take a second look at the broader tradition he represents.

Dr. Hauerwas' arguments are varied, and I will not address them exhaustively. However, the ones I will discuss fall into two roughly distinct types: contentions about the meaning of Jesus' message and the church, and contentions about natural law.

THE CHARACTER OF JESUS' LIFE

I take as the first example of the former type Dr. Hauerwas' comments that:

> What Lewis does not consider – an avoidance
> I fear that touches the heart of not only his
> understanding of pacifism but of his account
> of reason and Christianity – is that Christian
> nonviolence does not derive from any one
> dominical saying but from the very character
> of Jesus's life, death and resurrection.

---

http://www.abc.net.au/religion/articles/2012/08/24/3575360.htm (accessed on November 7, 2016) and in print with small changes as "On Violence," in *The Cambridge Companion to CS Lewis*, ed. Michael Ward (Cambridge: CUP, 2010): 189-201.

I have dealt in detail with specific exegetical arguments for pacifism in this book, and I won't repeat myself on that score. However, I would like to argue that the character of Jesus' life, death, and resurrection should be construed differently that Dr. Hauerwas suggests. These events do not support pacifism as he thinks they do.

Jesus' work on earth was to establish the kingdom of God. Of course, such a description raises as many questions as it answers. For hearers immediately want to know, what is the kingdom of God like? The name provides part of the answer: whatever it is, it is a sphere wherein God's will is done. He is the king in this kingdom. But the kingdom is not simply a place; it is also a time. Jesus makes this clear when he says in Luke 16:16 that the kingdom began after John, with Jesus' own ministry. So in some sense the kingdom of God was the time and place where the Creator was active through Jesus. Yet the Lord also spoke as if the kingdom were still future: he speaks of it as something the saints will inherit at the consummation (e.g., Matt 15:34). This raises the classic problem of "the now and the not yet", which brings us back to the matter at hand.

What does it look like, when the kingdom is present in the gospels? I hope I will not find disagreement when I suggest the following: it is present when people put their trust in Jesus, when they begin to live in a manner that accords with that faith, when Jesus heals their wounds and ailments, and when he casts out oppressive demons. In all such cases, the common denominator here is the activity of the Spirit in a manner beyond human control. No human being could simply decide to cause these effects on their own, and Jesus teaches this explicitly on a number of occasions: e.g., "without me you can do nothing," "the Spirit blows where it wishes," etc. But when the Spirit does come, people are healed internally, and though not in a permanent way like they experience in the eschaton, restored in their bodies and activity.

But what *doesn't* change when the kingdom comes in the gospels? Firstly, no holy land is demarcated for this kingdom. In fact, the logic seems to run in the opposite direction. Especially after his death and resurrection, it is clear that the kingdom of God will no longer be located in one geographical territory, but will fan out across the whole globe as God adds disciples to the church. Secondly, sin persists even within the visible church. If it did not, Jesus would have no need to teach his followers how to confess their own sins, nor how to deal with impenitent members of the community. Thirdly, princes and magistrates continue to exist on the earth. Though Jesus is installed as king of kings, he does not nullify civil government. Fourthly, all people, even believers, are still subject to the curse on the ground, and death.

In other words: the kingdom comes fundamentally into the hearts of believers, and expresses itself through Spirit-wrought works and wonders, but does not perfectly eliminate the presence of sin and its effects on the body and society. The rule of God is not perfectly expressed in the visible church. The church has no place of its own, no holy land, and so cannot be a kingdom in the strict sense; its people are still sojourners from God's presence, and have no territory to call their own as Christians *per se*. Further, sin still lives in them, and mortality still clings to their flesh. The rule of God expressed in perfect holiness and immortality still eludes them. And for these reasons, the kingdom does not obviate the need for authorities, and even for communal self-preservation in the face of threatening members.

And so Jesus' life, death, and resurrection do not really have the character of pacifism; what they have is the shape of the kingdom, which operates in a way different than the neo-Anabaptist vision suggests.

THE NOVELTY OF JESUS' MESSAGE

A second example of the Jesus-focused type of objection to Lewis' paper appears when Dr. Hauerwas writes:

> Accordingly, Jesus's authority is not expressed only in his teachings or his spiritual depth, but in "the way he went about representing a new moral option in Palestine, at the cost of his death." Christians are nonviolent not, therefore, because we believe that nonviolence is a strategy to rid the world of war, but because nonviolence is constitutive of what it means to be a disciple to Jesus.

To reiterate: Jesus' authority is said to be expressed in the "new moral option" he represented. But in what sense did Jesus claim to be presenting a new option in his teaching and example? At the beginning and end of his programmatic Sermon on the Mount, Jesus draws a line of continuity between the Law and the Prophets and his own moral teaching; the Lord was not in fact giving a "new and better" law than he did before his incarnation. It is true that Jesus went beyond the expectations of his contemporaries: in the same sermon he warns his listeners that they must do better than the Pharisees if they are to be subjects of God's kingdom. But note, this makes Jesus' teaching new relative to *the teachings of the Pharisees*, not God's revelation in nature or in the Old Testament. There are, no doubt, some changes in the shift from Old to New covenant. But in fact they all seem to be in the direction of simplification: a reduction in divine positive laws, and a return to something closer to the created order. Yet not quite: as noted before, the kingdom has not eliminated the presence of sin and death already, and the community of Jesus' disciples must reckon with this. These realities persisting, the age of the church is still more like the age of Noah and Moses than it is the Garden of Eden or the age to come.

THE RELEVANCE OF NATURAL LAW

Dr. Hauerwas later expresses concern about Prof. Lewis' relation of Christianity to natural law:

> Lewis, as is clear from his appeal to common sense, assumes a strong identification between what it means to be a Christian and what it means to be a human being.
>
> Throughout his work Lewis emphasized the difference being a Christian makes for what it means to believe in God, but how he understood that difference did not shape his thinking about war. I think he failed to draw out the implications of his theological convictions for war because of his conviction that a natural law ethic was sufficient to account for how we should think about war.

Lewis's flatfooted interpretation of "resist not evil" nicely illustrates his inability to recognize the difference Christ makes for the transformation of our "reason."

A little later he contends:

The problem is not in his account of the three elements of reason, but rather in his failure to see how reason and conscience must be transformed by the virtues. Such a view seems odd given his claim that though every moral judgment involves facts, intuitions, and reasoning, regard for authority commensurate with the virtue of humility is also required. That seems exactly right, but then I cannot help but wonder why Lewis does not include the lives of the martyrs as authorities for the shaping of Christian practical reason.

In "Learning in War-Time," Lewis observes that before he became a Christian he did not realize his life after conversion would consist in doing most of the same things he had done prior to his conversion. He notes that he hopes he is doing the same things in a new spirit, but they are still the same things. There is wisdom in what he says because we rightly believe that what it means to be a Christian is what God has created all to be. Therefore there is some continuity between the natural moral virtues and the theological virtues, but Lewis is wrong to think what he is doing is "the same thing." It cannot be the

same thing because what he "does" is part of
a different narrative.

The flaw in Prof. Lewis' account, then, is that he
separates practical reason from the character formation
of the reasoner, and in turn severs this shaping from the
distinctively Christian story. But in reality what people
take to be "reasonable" will be moulded by their habits
which form and are formed by their actions. And people
act in light of the narratives they tell themselves, so that
what they take to be ethically reasonable will flow from
these more fundamental stories. Dr. Hauerwas sees that
Prof. Lewis regarded facts, intuitions, reasoning, and
authorities as relevant to why people judge the way they
do, but thinks he failed to draw the correct conclusion on
this subject because he failed to take the right facts and
authorities—the specifically Christian ones, like the
martyrs—into account.

The appropriate rejoinder to Dr. Hauerwas follows
from all that I have said above. In fact, the gospels (the
Christian "narratives" if you will) present a story of a
redeemer coming to restore his created order, though not
all at once. Rather, he does it in stages, such that God
transforms the heart, and increasingly the character, now,
but leaves sin in the heart, the community, and the world
until the consummation. The community of the church,
then, is not a zone of perfect sinless separation from the
world; rather, it must deal with the same practical
problems the world does through its courts and
governments. Christianity claims to be the truth, and so
followers of Jesus must reason in light of what Jesus did
and taught because right reason submits to the truth. Yet
it does matter what Jesus in fact did and taught. It is only

if Jesus demanded pacifist practice that a "Christian reason" (a potentially misleading phrase, but we will go with it for the sake of argument) will necessarily shape habits and therefore actions in this direction.

Dr. Hauerwas raises the question of martyrs as authorities. What can be said about them? Well, consider this: if the gracious work of Christ has come to redeem nature, then it comes to uphold justice, since nature includes justice within it as it comes from the hand of God. But natural justice, when faced with violent injustice, includes justice in war. And a just war can only be waged if there is a reasonable prospect of success. Otherwise people are not seeking a justly ordered peace, but rather only their own deaths and those of others for no good effect. Yet the martyrs of the first through third centuries had no authority to wage war, nor did they have any reasonable prospect of success even if they did. If they had fought, then, they would have fallen foul of justice, and so nature, and thus would have opposed the character of Christ's grace. The behaviour of the martyrs, in other words, makes sense even on classical Protestant grounds, apart from pacifistic premises. Dr. Hauerwas might reply that most of these historical martyrs were actually pacifists in their own understanding, and he is probably right. But at this point the Protestant will reply: while admirable, the martyrs do not carry the authority of Jesus in the way that he or his apostles did. There was no promise to the martyrs that their teaching about doctrine and ethics would remain infallible. Rather, they are fallible defendants who must meet us at the same infallible judgment seat: the holy scriptures.

THE NECESSITY OF FORCE

Finally, Dr. Hauerwas questions whether Prof. Lewis' natural law reasoning is sound:

> Nor do pacifists have reason to disagree with Lewis's concern that the innocent be protected from homicidal maniacs. But there are nonviolent alternatives to protect innocent people from unjust attack. It is, moreover, quite a logical leap from using force to stop a homicidal maniac to justifying war. At best, Lewis has given a justification for the police function of governing authorities. But war is essentially a different reality than the largely peaceable work of the police.

At this point I could bring up ethical scenarios from imagination or history that might contradict this argument. If I could present even one such case where protecting the innocent would require violence, Dr. Hauerwas' argument would fail. That's because his point here seems to be violence is never practically necessary. There are always practically workable non-violent alternatives, he contends. But I am going to assume my readers are capable of coming up with such scenarios themselves. What I will note is a false assumption that often feeds into this pacifist counter, the idea that all people ultimately have a good will. That is, some pacifism assumes that all violent individuals can ultimately be reasoned with, and therefore that force is never really necessary. But this is simply not true, or at least we have no evidence to think it is. Violent sociopaths are people who violate this stricture: they are aware they hurt people, and that what they are doing is wrong, but they do it anyway. And scripture testifies that our experience is correct, that such rebellious people do exist. Those who have committed blasphemy against the Holy Spirit fall into this category, sinning as they do against the light. In the Old Testament, too, there was a known category of "high-handed" sins, which were defined by their wilfulness. So in fact there is no good reason to assume we can always talk violent people out of their behaviour, and that deep down they are all just folk like us. Sometimes they are not.

Dr. Hauerwas also contends that even if necessity could justify police violence, it would not follow that war was justified. He says these are not two realities on a continuum, but that they are qualitatively ("essentially") different. But, to borrow a phrase from Prof. Lewis, this will not answer. The logic of just war is the logic that underlies all political judgment: an authority effectively and proportionately discriminating between the right and the wrong, and establishing the former in the social order. The reality of war is that unintended injustice can be caused as a side-effect, but this is also true of police work. Collateral damage can occur in both military and police action. In fact the difference between the two kinds of judgments is this: military force works outside normal positive law constraints (since it expresses a conflict between two political communities), and happens on a larger scale. But both judgments are ultimately required by natural justice, which we perceive when we consider cases like the homicidal maniacs Dr. Hauerwas mentions.

Much more could be said about Dr. Hauerwas, Prof. Lewis, and their discussion about pacifism, but this will have to suffice for the present. Hopefully, though, the reader can see how Prof. Lewis' broad perspective, supplemented with some further exegetical and philosophical defense, remains a live option today for Christians thinking about the ethics of war.

BIBLIOGRAPHY

Allison, Dale C. *The Sermon on the Mount.* New York: Crossroad, 1999.

Bailey, Kenneth E. *Poet & Peasant and Through Peasant Eyes: A Literary-Cultural Approach to the Parables of Luke.* Grand Rapids: Eerdmans, 1983.

Bavinck, Herman. *Reformed Dogmatics: Prolegomena.* Grand Rapids: Baker Academic, 2003.

Burtchaell, James Tunstead. *From Synagogue to Church: Public Services and Offices in the Earliest Christian Communities.* Cambridge: CUP, 1992.

Bryan, Christopher. *Render to Caesar.* Oxford: OUP, 2005.

Carlston, Charles E. "Proverbs, Maxims, and the Historical Jesus." *Journal of Biblical Literature* 99, no.1 (1980): 87-105.

Collins, C. John. "Echoes of Aristotle in Romans 2:14–15: Or, Maybe Abimelech Was Not So Bad After All." *Journal of Markets & Morality* 13, no. 1 (2010): 123-173.

Day, John. *Crying for Justice: What the Psalms Teach us about Mercy and Vengeance in an Age of Terrorism.* Grand Rapids: Kregel Publications, 2005.

France, R.T. *The Gospel of Matthew.* New International Commentary on the New Testament. Grand Rapids: Eerdmans, 2007.

Gallant, Tim. *These Are Two Covenants: Reconsidering Paul on the Mosaic Law.* 2004; Grand Prairie, Alberta: Pactum Reformanda Publishing, 2012.

Gentry, Peter J. "Kingdom Through Covenant: Humanity as the Divine Image." *Southern Baptist Journal of Theology* 12, no. 1 [Spring 2008]: 26-28.

Grotius, Hugo. *The Rights of War and Peace.* Indianapolis: Liberty Fund, 2005. http://oll.libertyfund.org/titles/grotius-the-rights-of-war-and-peace-2005-ed-vol-1-book-i (accessed on October 14, 2016).

Hill, Charles. *Regnum Caelorum: Patterns of Millennial Thought in Early Christianity.* Oxford: OUP, 1992.

Instone-Brewer, David. *Divorce and Remarriage in the Bible: the Social and Literary Context.* Grand Rapids: Eerdmans, 2002.

Jones, Martin. "Semantic Axiom Number One." *Language* 48 (1972): 256-265.

Keener, Craig, S. *And Marries Another: Divorce and Remarriage in the Teaching of the New Testament.* Peabody: Hendrickson Publishers, 1991.

Lewis, C.S. *God in the Dock.* 1970; Grand Rapids: W.B. Eerdmans, 2014.

Lintamen, Stephen F. "The Pastoral Significance of the Anabaptist Vision." In *Refocusing a Vision: Shaping Anabaptist Character in the 21st Century.* [Goshen, IN: Mennonite Historical Society, 1995]. https://www.goshen.edu/mhl/Refocusing/DINTAMAN.htm (accessed September 30, 2016).

McGrath, Alistair. *Iustitia Dei: A History of the Christian Doctrine of Justification.* 3rd ed. Cambridge: CUP, 2005.

Nolland, John. *The New International Greek Commentary: The Gospel of Matthew.* Grand Rapids: Eerdmans, 2005.

O'Donovan, Oliver. *The Ways of Judgment.* Grand Rapids: Eerdmans, 2003.

Scaer, David P. "The Concept of Anfechtung in Luther's Thought." *Concordia Theological Quarterly* 47, no. 1 (Jan. 1983): 15-30.

Shillington, George. "Atonement Texture in 1 Corinthians." *Journal for the Study of the New Testament* 21 (1999): 29-50.

Sider, Ron. *The Early Church on Killing.* Grand Rapids: Baker Academic, 2012.

Sprinkle, Preston. *Fight: A Christian Case for Non-Violence.* Colorado Springs: David C. Cook, 2013.

Stott, John R. W. *The Cross of Christ: 20th Anniversary Edition.* Downer's Grove: InterVarsity Press, 2006.

Treat, Jeremy. *The Crucified King: Atonement and Kingdom in Biblical and Systematic Theology.* Grand Rapids: Zondervan, 2014.

Vidu, Adonis. *Atonement, Law, and Justice: The Cross in Historical and Cultural Contexts.* Grand Rapids: Baker Academic, 2014.

Welty, Greg. "The Eschatological Fulfillment and Confirmation of Mosaic Law: A Response to D.A. Carson and Fred Zaspel on Matthew 5:17-48." Analogical Thoughts: The Virtual Home of James N. Anderson. Last modified March 28, 2002. http://www.proginosko.com/welty/carson.htm (accessed on August 13, 2016).

Wright, N.T. "Romans." In *The New Interpreter's Bible: Acts – First Corinthians*, vol. 10. Nashville, TN: Abington, 2002.

Yoder, John Howard. *Nevertheless: The Varieties of Religious Pacifism*. Waterloo, Ontario: Herald Press, 1992.

_____. *The Original Revolution: Essays on Christian Pacifism*. Waterloo, Ontario: Herald Press, 2003).

_____. *The Politics of Jesus*. Grand Rapids: Eerdmans, 1972.

Zanchi, Girolamo. *On the Law in General*. Sources in Early Modern Economics, Ethics, and Law, translated by Jeffrey J. Veenstra. Grand Rapids: CLP Academic, 2012.

DATE DUE

58704761R00071

Made in the USA
Lexington, KY
19 December 2016